Walks in ...

Cheshire AND Wirral

Walks IN
Mysterious
Cheshire AND Wirral

Circular walks through Cheshire and
Wirral's historic countryside

Tony Bowerman

Northern Eye

First published in 1990 by Thistle Books, Wirral.

This wholly revised and updated edition published in 2006 by

Northern Eye Books
Castleview, High Street,
Tattenhall,
Cheshire CH3 9PX.

Reprinted 2009

www.northerneyebooks.com

ISBN 0 9553557 0 2
ISBN 978 0 9553557 0 7

For sales enquiries, please telephone: 01928 723 744

Northern Eye Books Limited Reg. No. 05460709

A CIP catalogue record for this book is available from the British Library.

Whilst every effort has been made to ensure that the information in this book
is correct at the time of publication, neither the author nor the publisher can
accept any responsibility for any errors, loss or injury, however caused.

The routes described in this book are undertaken at the individual's own
risk. The publisher and copyright owners accept no responsibility for any
consequences arising from the use of this book, including misinterpretation
of the maps and directions.

Maps based on out of copyright Ordnance Survey mapping, aerial
photographs and local knowledge.

Printed and bound in Great Britain by Cromwell Press Group, Wiltshire.

"Anything that adds mystery to Cheshire history is to be applauded. If variety spices life then the 14 walks in this book certainly unearth the essential spice of life in Cheshire.

Tony Bowerman has produced a book you can walk around physically with maps to help you. Or you can take a stroll in your imagination through such mysteries as the ghostly duck or gypsy king's grave. Or if you want to be really lazy you can sit in your armchair and imagine Neston Quay in the 16th century. 'A solitary inn stood close to the shore at this remote spot. A map of 1599 shows a wooden house that later became a prison for smugglers, runaway servants and religious recusants.'

Mysterious? You bet.

Now read on. **"**

— PATRICK O'NEILL, EDITOR OF **'CHESHIRE LIFE'**

Acknowledgements

Writing a book involves the help of many people. In particular, I'd like to thank the staff of Chester Reference Library, Cheshire Records and Archives, Cheshire County Council's 'Revealing the Past' team and County Historic Environment Record, Bollington Civic Society, The National Trust, Manchester Museum, The Peckforton Hills Local Heritage Initiative, the Shocklach churchwardens, and several residents of Willington's Gooseberry Lane.

Photographs

Carl Rogers, John Street, Cheshire Records and Archives, The National Trust, Bollington Civic Society, Chester Archaeological Society, Peckforton Hills Local Heritage Initiative, Tom Wright.

Contents

Introduction *9*
What is so Mysterious about Cheshire? Rights of Way; Other
public access; Access Land; Maps; The Countryside Code.

Map of Cheshire and Wirral and location of the walks *13*

1. **Parkgate and Neston**: *Along the Changing Shore* *14*
    Disused railway line, Neston quay, Neston colliery, Denhall
    quay, silted up estuary, Parkgate promenade, reedbeds and
    nature reserve.

2. **Little Barrow**: *Across the Gowy Marshes* *27*
    Hilltop settlement, sunken green lanes, across the flatlands,
    the River Gowy, ancient farm, isolated Plemstall Church,
    Saint Plegmund's Well, footbridges and local memories.

3. **Hockenhull Platts**: *Packhorse Bridges over the River Gowy* .. *37*
    Ancient packhorse route, raised causeway across the
    marshes, marshy nature reserve, three medieval packhorse
    bridges, quiet riverside paths, old watermill, and a section
    of Roman Watling Street.

4. **Shocklach**: *Around Castletown* *46*
    Isolated Norman church, ancient cross, ghostly procession,
    shifting river, medieval lanes, Norman castle mound and
    ditches, Roman road, lost medieval settlement.

5. **Willington**: *Above 'Little Switzerland'* *56*
    Hidden valley, shelf-like path, Iron Age hillfort, Ice Age
    meltwater gorge and pleasant views.

6. **Delamere**: *Along Roman Watling Street, below the Hillfort* ... *64*
    Iron Age and Saxon hillfort, Roman roads, medieval quarry,
    and round the 'Old Pale'.

7. **Peckforton**: *From the Stone Elephant to The Pheasant* *75*
    Cheshire's own 'Elephant and Castle', cobbled estate track,
    ancient saltway over the hills, haunted bridge, panoramic
    views and a Gospel Oak.

8. **Bickerton**: *From Mad Allen's Hole to Maiden Castle*.............. 83
Hermit's cave, memorial stone, Iron Age hillfort, views, breezes and bilberries.

9. **Tushingham**: *A Dead Duck and Diploma* 93
Ancient half-timbered inn, ghostly duck, Cavalier's hat, isolated chapel and horse drawn hearse, lost Roman and medieval roads, rare Roman bronze diploma, and a bottomless pit.

10. **Little Budworth**: *The Remains of* Mondrum 103
Ancient commonland, sunken paths, mill pool, Romanies' meeting place, and the grave of the 'King of the Gypsies'.

11. **Whitegate**: *Where Vale Royal Abbey stood* 111
Picturesque village, Nun's Grave and ghost, site of Vale Royal Abbey, wooded Weaver Valley, and prophesies of Nixon—the Cheshire seer.

12. **Lindow Moss**: *In Search of the Bog Man* 120
Lindow Common and Black Lake, Lindow Moss, peat cutters, and two 'bog burials'—Iron Age sacrificial victims preserved in the peat.

13. **Alderley Edge**: *Across the Copper Hills* 132
Legend of the Wizard of Alderley Edge, Bronze Age copper mines, Engine Vein, Stormy Point, Devil's Grave, Saddle Bole, Holy Well, Armada Beacon, Castle Rock, Wizard's Well, caves and hidden mine entrances.

14. **Bollington**: *From 'White Nancy' along Kerridge Ridge* 143
'White Nancy', beacon site, Kerridge Stone quarries, fossils, Peaks and Plains, coal pits and flag-stoned footpath.

Further Reading 156
About the Author 158

Introduction

What is so Mysterious about Cheshire?

IN THE BALM OF SUMMER or on a crisp winter's day, I sometimes sit of one of Cheshire's higher hills—Beeston Crag, Helsby Hill, or Congleton Cloud—and gaze out over the plain. From such a vantage point a single question always delights me: What did the landscape stretched out below look like in the distant past?

How much was forest and how much marsh? Where did the old tracks and roadways run? Where were the first small settlements, villages and towns? What *did* the changing face of Cheshire look like to our ancestors?

Yet all the clues are there in our modern, increasingly ephemeral landscape. Clues that will tell us how things used to be. They are only waiting to be uncovered. And by walking in that landscape with our eyes and minds open to the past, we can take a closer look. *Walks in Mysterious Cheshire and Wirral* is just that: an attempt to trace Cheshire's hazy past, to explore the last hidden corners, and to wring out the remnants of a vanishing way of life—old Cheshire—before the pace of change removes them forever. Take that chance while you may, because the countryside will soon be altered beyond all recognition.

Rights of Way

Public footpaths are a very British feature; with over 120,00 miles/192,000 kilometres of public paths in England and Wales, we have more than any other country. In Scotland, walkers enjoy even greater freedom of access. While in places such as Sweden and Switzerland, the public have the right to wander where they please in the countryside, subject only to local laws and the understanding that no damage is done.

So the English or Welsh footpath is both a freedom and a restriction. In Britain, all land is owned by someone—an individual or a corporate body—and the walker often has to keep to specific routes and rights of way.

A Right of Way (ROW) is just that: a right to cross someone's land. The landowner may properly object if the walker does damage or leaves litter. If a walker strays from the right of way, he or she is trespassing and may be asked to leave by the most direct route, or sued for damages.

There are several kinds of right of way:

- **Public footpaths** provide a right of way for walkers—often waymarked in yellow;

- **Bridleways** provide a right of way for walkers, horse riders and cyclists—often waymarked in blue;

- **Restricted Byways** provide a right of way for walkers, horse riders, cyclists and other non-mechanically propelled vehicles;

- **Byways** provide a right of way for all traffic.

However, the Rights of Way shown on Ordnance Survey maps are taken from the definitive maps held by local authorities and may be subject to changes and amendments. If in doubt, ask to see your local authority's definitive maps.

Other Public Access
Other routes with public access include:

- **National Trails** and **Long Distance Routes**;

- **Traffic Free Cycle Routes**;

- **National Cycle Routes**;

- **Permitted footpaths** and **permitted bridleways**—where the landowner allows public use but retains the right to withdraw that permission—are not rights of way.

The curious sandstone elephant and castle at Peckforton

Access Land

Walkers have long campaigned for the right to roam across wide-open spaces.

The Countryside and Rights of Way Act 2000 introduced a new right for people to walk, responsibly and subject to some common sense restrictions, over areas of open countryside and registered common land in England and Wales.

Access Land also includes land managed by the National Trust, the Forestry Commission, and the Woodland Trust.

Access land is now shown on the OS Explorer series maps by a yellow tint edged with orange. For updates and more information, see: www.countrysideaccess.gov.uk.

Maps

The best maps for exploring Cheshire are those published by the Ordnance Survey. Two sets of maps at different scales show Cheshire's public rights of way. The silver and magenta covered 1:50,000 **Landranger** series covers most of Cheshire in three maps; while the orange covered 1:25,000 **Explorer** series shows almost all of Cheshire in seven; with just three core maps: 257, 266, 267.

While both series are useful, walkers, cyclists and horse riders will find the extra detail and field boundaries shown on the Explorer maps invaluable. Many Explorer maps are double sided, and all show the entire public rights of way network, as well as permissive paths and access land.

The Countryside Code

The simplified Countryside Code reflects new open access rights and social changes over the last 20 or so years.

- Be safe—plan ahead and follow any signs
- Leave gates and property as you find them
- Protect plants and animals, and take your litter home
- Keep dogs under close control
- Consider other people

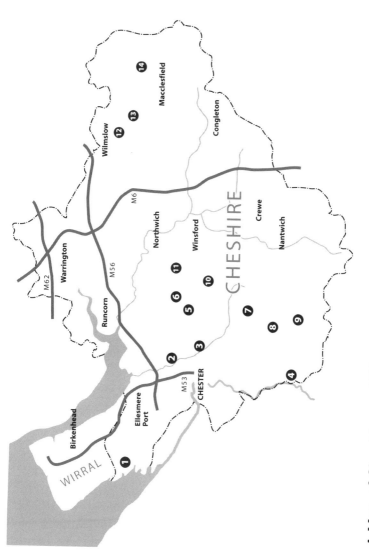

A Map of Cheshire and Wirral showing the location of the walks

1. Parkgate and Neston

Along the Changing Shore

Disused railway line, Neston quay, Neston colliery, Denhall quay, silted up estuary, Parkgate promenade, reedbeds and nature reserve

Start: *Wirral Way car park, on the B5135 Neston-Parkgate road, at the southern end of Parkgate. Map reference: SJ 283779.*

Distance: *4½ miles/7 kilometres.*

Duration: *Allow 2½-3 hours.*

Difficulty: *Easy. Almost flat: surfaced, disused railway line; field and shoreline paths; and Parkgate promenade. Muddy in places.*

Food and Drink: *Harp Inn, Quayside, Little Neston. Timothy Taylors and Holt cask ales. Homemade hot and cold food. Pub games. Beer garden and shore-side tables. 0151 336 6980. OR: Numerous pubs and cafes in Parkgate.*

Maps: *OS 1:25,000 Explorer 266 Wirral and Chester/Caer; OS 1:50,000 Landranger 117 Chester & Wrexham.*

NESTON AND PARKGATE look out from the Wirral peninsula across the open expanse of the Dee Estuary: Cheshire's last, vast, undervalued wilderness. Yet each year the estuary is shrinking.

In fact, it's been silting up ever since the Middle Ages. Today, the panorama across to the Welsh shore spans 12,750 hectares/31,500 acres and stretches for 20 kilometres/12 miles from Hilbre island at the estuary's mouth to Shotton steelworks. But until the early fifteenth century, the estuary pushed inland for 32 kilometres/20 miles, right up to the Port of Chester—then the most important seaport in England, after London and Bristol. The course of the river was different too, curving out past Blacon Point, Shotwick Castle and Burton Point, along the Wirral shore.

Troops and government officials sailed out to Ireland, and ships brought cloth from Flanders, linen from Germany, and wine from France and Spain in on the tide. But the river was changing. By 1486, the problems of the River Dee were referred to in a royal document as, *'a vehement influx of sand, and a silting up of gravel'*. In those days, remedial measures were out of the question. There was neither the money nor the technology. So the port was shifted lower and lower down the estuary: first to Shotwick, then to Burton, Denhall, Neston, and finally to Parkgate.

This ad hoc solution worked for the next 200 years or so, until silt encroached on Parkgate, too. Then, between 1732 and 1737, a new channel was cut from Chester to Connor's Quay on the

Children playing on a beached sailing vessel at Parkgate around 1910

Welsh side of the estuary. Though the county boundary still followed the river's old course, the Dee itself had been artificially moved over to the Welsh shore. A sluice near Chester joined the new channel to the old river. But without its tidal flow, the old river was dead. The canalisation allowed a series of embankments to reclaim part of the marsh, thus creating valuable farmland—the aptly named Sealand.

The most ambitious embankment of all was intended to stretch from Burton to Connah's Quay on the far shore. But, breached by high tides in 1877 and known thereafter as the Broken Bank, it was finished only in 1916; today, it's usually known as Burton Cop. The estuary had been radically altered. In the short term, 5000 hectares/19 square miles of saltmarsh and mud had been reclaimed for farmland and profit. But in the long term, the consequences were dire.

Spartina cordgrass, introduced from America to stabilise the Dee banks at Connah's Quay in 1928, rapidly colonised the new mudflats, speeding the natural development of saltmarsh. As the sea was pushed back, the estuary shrank. To compound these losses, the estuary is still viewed as expendable wasteland today rather than as a priceless wilderness. Industrial waste is tipped on the marsh. Houses, roads and industry encroach on the shore. Sadly, it seems certain that the Dee estuary of the next century will be a different and a poorer place.

The walk

The walk begins at the Wirral Country Park's 'Wirral Way' car park, on the B5135 Neston-Parkgate road, at the southern end of Parkgate.

Less than 500 metres from the seafront, the car park occupies the first high ground above the estuary. Notice the concrete World War Two machine gun nest, or 'pillbox', beside the parking area, guarding the road as it rises from the shore.

1. From the car park, go through a gap beside a gate and head south on the broad, limestone-grit surfaced Wirral Way. It's waymarked by a black footprint on a circular yellow background. This is also 'Location 56' on the 'National Cycle Network' and the Wirral Way is popular with cyclists as well as walkers and horse riders.

Running parallel with the foot and cycle way is a sandy bridleway dedicated to horses; both occupy the former trackbed of the disused Hooton-to-West Kirby railway. Opened in 1866, it was an offshoot of the main Chester-to-Birkenhead line. For seven of the line's twelve miles the track ran close to the Wirral shore. Steam trains brought townspeople out to Parkgate and the seaside on Cheap Day Excursions, and took back to the

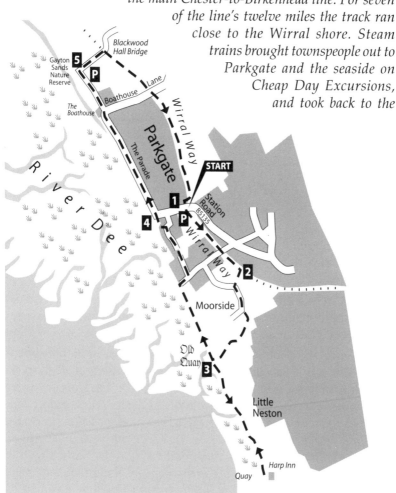

cities Wirral's early potatoes, rattling milk churns, and coal from Neston's collieries. But by 1962 the line was closed. The seaside resorts had silted up, the collieries were shut, and the farms were slowly being covered with houses. For a while the line lay derelict. But in 1973, backed by money from the government's Countryside Commission, and after a great deal of work, the old railway line was opened as Wirral Country Park. It was the first Country Park in Britain. Today, the old track is filled with birdsong rather than the rush of engines; while wildflowers flourish uncut on the cuttings and embankments.

Within 400 metres, the Wirral Way passes under a solid sandstone bridge beneath Moorside Lane.

It was from near here that the old 'mineral line' curved down to the Wirral Colliery at Ness Holt, beside the shore at Little Neston. Opened in 1877, it was built to carry coal from the Neston collieries for use across mainland Britain. Now disused and swallowed up by fields, the original route of the line can still be traced clearly on the OS Explorer map.

Walk on along the Wirral Way. Continue past a clearly signposted footpath between Neston and Moorside.

2. Three hundred metres later, turn right, through a wooden kissing gate, on a footpath across the fields. When the path forks, almost immediately, keep straight ahead on the main, right-hand footpath towards the shore.

Soon the path crosses the overgrown branch line to Ness Holt, hemmed in on either side by tall hedges. Go straight on, across another field, to emerge through a metal kissing gate on narrow, unsurfaced Old Quay Lane.

For centuries, what is now Old Quay Lane provided the only access to the New Key (now called the Old Quay!) at Neston. Passengers embarking or disembarking by sailing ship for Ireland travelled along the lane by coach on their way to and from Chester. The winding lane provided the sole road access to the quay, sandwiched between the shoreline marshes, or 'Moors', at Moorside, and one of Neston's communal Town Fields on the inland side. Alternatively, foot passengers could walk, carrying their baggage, along the same, more direct footpath we've just taken, from Neston Church to the Quay.

Turn left along the lane. Almost immediately, the path veers sharp right, and heads across the fields towards the shore. Beyond a boggy area, a wooden footbridge crosses a stream as it meanders to the sea. Two fields later, with Moel Famau clear on the horizon directly ahead, the path opens suddenly onto the broad expanse of the Dee Estuary. Well-worn steps in a sandstone wall on the edge of the marsh lead to the ruins of Neston Old Quay.

It's a lovely place, dominated by sky and wind. The view is filled with constant movement: tall sea grass combed out in the breeze, swirling seabirds and a ceaseless procession of clouds.

The 'ness' element in Neston's name is an Anglo-Saxon word meaning a nose or headland. For thousands of years, a long spit of land jutted into the tide here; a fact corroborated by Speed's map of 1611. So when ships were first unable to reach Chester as the Dee silted up, this 'ness' seemed a godsend—a natural quay at which to load and unload. Sheltered behind it was 'Lightfoot's Pool', *deep enough to be* 'in the belly of the sea'.

Work on building a stone quay at the 'New Haven' began in 1541, though because of lack of money it wasn't completed for another forty years. The hey-day of Neston Key—as it was then known—was during the 17th century. The historian William Webb wrote in 1622 that the quay was, 'where our passengers to Ireland do so often lie awaiting the pleasure of the winds, which make many people better acquainted with the place than they desire to be'. *But as the 'Port of Chester' declined, and Liverpool gained a reputation as more than a fishing creek, the quay was finally abandoned. Neston Quay is hardly mentioned after the 1690s. In 1779 the ruins were sold to local landowner Sir Roger Mostyn and much of the stone reused to build the sea wall at Parkgate. At one time the depth of water off Neston Quay was over 10 metres/30 feet at spring tides; today the area is essentially dry land.*

In the past, a solitary inn stood close to the shore at this remote spot. A map of 1599 shows a wooden house that later became a prison for smugglers, runaway servants, and religious recusants. Rebuilt in brick in the 1680s as the 'Key House' inn, the former prison soon became

Miners coming off the final shift at Wirral Colliery in 1926

popular with travellers. One wrote, 'We made a very fayre passage, and landed at Nesson about seven at night, and lay at the Key House, at George Eaton's'. *Strangely, in 1902 local colliers discovered a secret hiding place in the ruined chimney—perhaps once used by smugglers to conceal contraband. No trace of the inn remains today.*

3. Facing out over the estuary, turn left at the Old Quay, along the shore towards Little Neston. The path follows the tideline along the rim of the marsh. Four hundred metres later, a reedbed hugs the shore where fresh water springs trickle into the marsh. Soon the path climbs back onto firm ground to join a surfaced track. Up to the left are the last spoil heaps of the old Neston Collieries.

The track emerges at a broad turning area at the bottom of Marshlands Road. Walk on, past modern bungalows to the Harp Inn and Denhall Quay.

Like much of the Wirral, Ness and Neston were originally Viking settlements; and the name Denhall derives from Danewell, *meaning a favourite watering place for ships.*

Wirral Colliery

The first shafts at Wirral Colliery were sunk around 1760, and in their prime there were 90 pits between Neston and Denhall. Burdett's map of 1777 shows *'Coal Pits'* at Denhall. Based on an arm of the North Wales coalfield, the Wirral Colliery's coal was of poor quality and much of it went for steam coal to feed steamship boilers.

The levels ran up to 3 kilometres/2 miles out under the estuary; and, not surprisingly, the mines were often half flooded. The seam of coal was only two feet thick in places and conditions were almost unbelievably harsh. Coal dust, seawater, cold and rats meant the life expectancy of a Wirral miner was shorter than that of a contemporary plantation slave.

During the winter, the miners seldom saw the sun for months on end. So it's not surprising that when the mines closed in 1926, some of the miners went on to become shepherds, wildfowlers and fishermen—livelihoods in sharp contrast to their old jobs underground.

Most of the old colliery workings and spoil heaps are now buried under new housing estates. However, the last remaining spoil tip, now deeply furrowed by almost a century of rain, rises 15 metres above the shore. Gorse and broom are already colonising the top—their flowers yellow against the black.

The slight elevation of the summit emphasises the size and openness of the estuary. Gutters multiply and the sands of the Dee are visible across the saltings. And sometimes, in the heat of summer, Hilbre and the pitheads of the old Point of Air colliery near Prestatyn are islands hanging in the air —mirages cut off from the anchoring ground like images from a fairytale.

The out-of-the-way Harp Inn overlooks the estuary. Originally known as the 'Welch Harp' and the 'Old Harp Inn', this remote pub was once a favourite drinking place for wildfowlers and the Lancashire, Staffordshire and Welsh miners brought in to work at Neston Colliery.

Nearby is Denhall Quay, built in the 1760s to load Neston coal for export, mainly to coal-less Ireland and the Isle of Man—in the days before the silting up of the Denhall Gutter stopped barges coming alongside. Without this cheap transport, the collieries were no longer viable; and the last coal barges docked here in the 1850s. Old locals also know the stone jetty as Lawton's Quay, after a well-known wildfowler and punt builder called William Lawton, who built himself a house on the derelict quay. Many of the quay's sandstone blocks have since tumbled, and a few wind-stunted hawthorn bushes and sycamores grow on the jetty. It's a good place to sit and take in the view towards Burton Point and Shotton.

From Denhall Quay, turn back along the shore to Neston Old Quay. Return over the sandstone steps in the wall, and turn immediately left, on along the shore towards Parkgate. Within 100 metres, a narrow wooden footbridge crosses a stream that runs out into the marsh.

Nearby are the last remnants of the quay: a wall of huge sandstone blocks eroded by ancient seawater.

Two fields later, the grassy path drops down to the shore again, and crosses a waymarked stile beside a wall and hawthorn hedge.

A line of springs flowing into the marsh here supports the huge Neston reedbed—superb habitat for small, elusive birds like warblers and reed buntings.

In summer, the reeds tower overhead and the path skirts the marsh in a natural green tunnel. Some 500 metres later, the path emerges at a broad grassy area above the estuary. Houses block further easy progress along the shore, and the signposted public footpath turns inland for a while. Within 50 metres, turn left along 'Manorial Road South' past bungalows with winsome nautical names like 'Whitewings' and 'The Anchorage'.

At the end of the road, a narrow path runs briefly between

Cockle fishermen unloading at Parkgate's Middle Slip in the 1930s

high fences to emerge on another quiet suburban street. When this road kinks sharply to the right, 250 metres on, turn left, down a narrow footpath alongside the brick boundary wall of large 'Riverside' house. Shortly afterwards, the path opens onto the breezy estuary once more.

4. Turn right, along the top of the sandstone sea wall to gain the southern end of Parkgate promenade. For the next kilometre our route follows the seafront with Parkgate's cafes, pubs and shops crowded along one side, facing out over the Dee Estuary.

Walk on past black and white Mostyn House School—an 'Independent Day School for Boys and Girls Aged 4-18'.

In the seventeenth century, the huge roots and trunks of a submerged forest, similar to that once visible at Meols, could be seen along the shore here. *Fossilised animal teeth have also been picked up on the beach.*

Parkgate today is an unusual and delightful place. Yet until the eighteenth century, it was little more than a straggle of houses beside the gate of the King's deer park. When the 'New Cut' diverted the Dee away to the Welsh side of the estuary in 1737, Neston and Denhall quays' days were numbered. As they gradually silted up, Parkgate rose to prominence. From the 1680s until around 1815, Parkgate 'partook of all the importance and bustle of a sea port, and packets and other vessels were employed here in the trade with Ireland'. *The preacher, John Wesley often sailed from Parkgate. Only a few years later, the water was too shallow for the Dublin packet, and Parkgate was finished as a port. By 1830, Pigot's Directory concludes,* 'Parkgate is of importance only as being the resort of visitors to it in the bathing season.'

An early visitor in 1784 was Emma, Lady Hamilton, perhaps the most famous beauty of Georgian times and mistress to Lord Nelson. Seawater was widely prescribed as a tonic in the eighteenth century, both for bathing and drinking, and she came here to cure a persistent skin problem. Women often bathed naked but Emma hired a horse-drawn 'bathing van' and bathing dress along with a 'woman dipper' to ensure she got fully wet without drowning. Even as late as the 1880s, it was still customary to carry children down to the sea wrapped in a blanket, dip them three times in the sea, before carrying them back to bed. Old photographs show Victorian and Edwardian children playing happily on Parkgate's broad sandy beach. Parkgate remained popular as a seaside resort until the 1930s; and only in the 1950s did the marsh finally blanket Parkgate sands.

Continue along Parkgate promenade past 'The Ship Hotel', 'Nichol's Famous Ice-Cream' and the 'Lobster Grill'.

Roughly half way along the Parade, beyond Mostyn Square, is Mealor's Fresh Seafoods selling 'Fresh Parkgate Shrimps', rather than the 'Parkgate Fresh Shrimps' sold elsewhere—a subtle but vital difference. During the 1920s, Parkgate shrimps, cockles and mussels were sold to day-trippers in tearooms along the Parade; while tons more were sent off by rail to Liverpool and the Lancashire towns. But by the late 1960s and early '70s, silting up of the estuary and increasing pollution had killed off the shrimping industry.

The road narrows beside the Old Watch House at the end of the Parade.

Opposite is the Middle Slip where Parkgate fishermen once unloaded baskets of shrimps, and sacks of cockles and mussels at high tide. The shellfish were carried home by pony and cart for cleaning and sorting. Today, with the marsh hard against the seawall, it's hard to appreciate that two-masted sailing yawls, and later 'nobbies', once crowded the slip.

Walk on beside the marsh to the Boat House pub at the bottom of Boathouse Lane.

Until the northern end of the Parade was built in 1840, Boathouse Lane ran straight down to the river and the deep-water mooring of Beerhouse Hole. There was an inn here from 1613 onwards, known at different times as the Beerhouse or Ferry House. A French traveller in the 1660s called the area, 'the little village of Birhouse, eight miles from [Chester]', *and recorded,* 'Here are some large storehouses for the keeping of merchandise to be embarked for Ireland.' *The inn was later known as the Pengwern Arms. During the 1800s, it was the arrival and departure point for ferries to Bagillt and Flint across the estuary in North Wales. Horse drawn coaches met the ferry to take passengers to Liverpool and Chester.*

Continue along the shore on the tarmaced lane beside the black and white Boat House pub. It's signposted to 'Gayton 1 mile'. Ahead is Wirral Country Park's 'Old Baths Car Park'.

The car park was originally the site of a tidal saltwater swimming pool, which was closed in 1942 as the estuary progressively silted up.

The Old Baths car park and nearby shore are a nature lover's heaven. The marshes here come wildly alive with each of the year's twenty or so high 'spring tides'. Voles, water shrews and as many as 300 water rails, concentrated by the rising water, lure herons and other hunters in to feed. Wildfowl and waders wing in up the gutters and over the margins of the marsh in their thousands. To see the build up of birds towards high water, it's best to arrive 1½-2 hours before the tide. Tides of nine metres and over concentrate the flocks; while a ten metre tide results in loss of the whole foreshore. For tidal details, buy an inexpensive book of tables from one of Parkgate's shops. It's one of Cheshire's natural wonders and not to be missed.

5. At the far end of the car park, turn right, through a gate, away from the shore; the path is signposted for the 'Wirral Way'. At the top of the gentle slope, 200 metres later, cross the old brick railway bridge and turn right, down steps to rejoin the Wirral Way. Go left at the bottom of the steps, away from the bridge.

The disused railway line is quiet and edged with hawthorn, oak and wildflowers.

Continue through the bridge beneath Boathouse Lane. Some 500 metres later, the Wirral Way crosses blue-painted Brooklands Road Bridge beside a school. When the track meets the B5135, turn right, along busy Station Road.

Parkgate Station once stood nearby. Built in 1866, it had a subway beneath the lines connecting the wooden platforms on either side.

Beyond the roadside sign for 'Parkgate', turn left, back into the Wirral Way car park and the end of the walk.

2. Little Barrow

Across the Gowy Marshes

Hilltop settlement, sunken green lanes, across the flatlands, the River Gowy, ancient farm, isolated Plemstall Church, St. Plegmund's Well, footbridges, and local memories

Start: *Little Barrow 4 miles/6.5 kilometres east of Chester. Map reference: SJ 470699.*

Distance: *3 miles/5 kilometres.*

Duration: *Allow 2 hours.*

Difficulty: *Mostly flat; one descent and one ascent. Green lanes, farm tracks, and field paths; muddy at times.*

Food and Drink: *The Foxcote, Station Lane, Little Barrow. Pub and seafood restaurant. Children welcome. 01244 301343.*

Maps: *OS 1:25,000 Explorer 266 Wirral and Chester/Caer; OS 1:50,000 Landranger 117 Chester, Wrexham and surrounding area.*

TRAVELLERS BY BOAT UP THE MERSEY IN PRE-ROMAN TIMES would have seen a deeply cut bay on the southern shore where Cheshire's River Gowy pushed its waters out into the tide. Most of them paddled on to enter the Weaver, for landing before that on the Cheshire bank was virtually impossible. The slow-flowing Gowy falls only 280 feet/90 metres from its source beneath the Peckforton Hills, and much of its lower course was a broad, waterlogged marshland, extending inland to what is now Huxley, and beyond.

A maze of streams, swamp and peat moss, the Gowy marshes effectively cut northern Cheshire in half. Willows and water-loving alders fringed the vast wind-combed reed-beds full of ducks, geese, bitterns and herons; eels and otters coexisted in the gutters, and harriers quartered the marshes on the lookout for unwary prey. It was a wilderness teeming with life; it was also a wilderness ripe with possibility for mankind.

Settlements grew up on each scrap of high ground. The name Ince—an ancient village near the Gowy's mouth—comes from the Welsh *ynys* meaning island. Elton, Thornton and Stoak were other early settlements. While Plemstall—*Plegmund's Stow*, the hermitage of Plegmund—was another island that probably hosted an Anglo-Saxon wooden church during the Dark Ages. Equally remote was the Norman abbey at Stanlow, near the Gowy's mouth; but in 1279 and again in 1287 it was flooded out, the buildings submerged and access by land cut off. In response to piteous appeals, the Pope moved the monks to Lancashire. Living amidst the Gowy Marshes was never easy.

The walk

The walk begins at the hilltop village of Little Barrow, 4 miles/7 kilometres north-east of Chester, overlooking the broad flood-plain of the Gowy. The name Barrow comes from the Old English

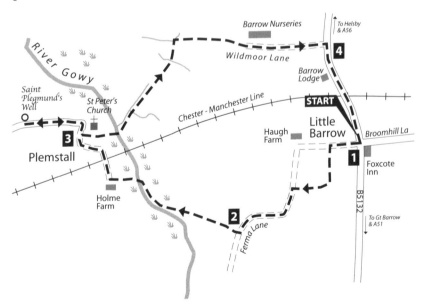

word *beorg* meaning hill. Turn off the A 51 Chester to Manchester road onto the B5132, not far from Chester at Stamford Bridge. A mile beyond Great Barrow, park close to The Foxcote, a white-painted pub restaurant perched on the edge of the slope at Broomhill.

Once known affectionately as 'The Snig' after the Cheshire dialect word for an eel—which in the past were abundant in the nearby Gowy—the pub is still sometimes called by another of its old names, The Railway. It stands on Station Lane. It's been a pub since about 1850, before which it was 'Three dwelling houses with gardens and outbuildings'. *Until 1914 the landlord and his wife would let out spare bedrooms to visitors holidaying in the countryside from Lancashire's industrial towns.*

1. Directly opposite the pub, a rough lane drops downhill between sandstone-walled banks topped with hawthorn.

Worn down 6 feet/2 metres into the bedrock in places, the lane is old. Look at the exposed sandstone—in places you can see the aptly named Bunter Pebble Beds made up of pebbles lain down in a river delta during the Triassic period some 200 million years ago.

From a gate at a bend in the lane the view opens out over the broad flood plain of the River Gowy. Beyond, the Welsh mountains stretch along the horizon in a pastel backdrop. Away to the right are the storage tanks, tall stacks and orange flares of Stanlow Oil Refinery. Primarily to prevent flood damage to this modern installation, the Gowy's river bed has been substantially lowered and the marshes drained. Now black and white dairy cattle dot the dike-crossed pastures—a dull modern substitute for reeds and water.

Shortly after the gate, and about 200 metres from the pub, go up a steep flight of stone steps in the hedgerow to the left. From the top of the steps, the path skirts the field edge ahead, before following the hedge downhill to the right. The path then joins the rough farm track called Ferma Lane, which runs along the contour of the slope towards Great Barrow.

The curious name of this ancient lane comes from the Old English

A horse-drawn plough in fields at Barrow in the 1930s

fenn, *meaning fen or marsh. Originally, the lane ran along the rim of the marsh; a look at the contours confirms this supposition. That the lane is old is supported by the large variety of tree species along its length, among them: oak, hawthorn, blackthorn, hazel, ash and elder. A survey of hedges in the parish in 1977 calculated Ferma Lane to be at least 500 years old.*

2. The lane kinks to the right, then bears left. About 150 metres further on, turn right over a stile beside a large field gate, off Ferma Lane and into the fields. The flat ground ahead was once enveloped by the Gowy Marshes.

Centuries ago Ferma Lane followed the margin of the mire, where the willows and alders ended and a sea of reeds began. At this point the marshes were half-a-mile/1 kilometre wide, and stretched across to Mickle Trafford; downstream towards the Mersey Estuary they were far broader. Imagine the wind soughing across thousands of acres of upright, raffia-hued stems.

The fertility of the rich alluvial soil in the river valley has long been recognised; the problem was to drain it. By the early 14th century half a dozen dikes had been built towards Frodsham, and in the 1340s a scheme to build a giant sluice to prevent winter flooding failed when the timbers were swept away by winter storms. Reclamation of the marshes was always an expensive business, but after the Black Death had drastically reduced the population, work stopped for a while.

Cross a simple railway-sleeper bridge over a deep drain and set out straight across the following field, heading for the farm buildings of Holme Farm.

Passing the low concrete parapet of another deep drainage ditch that runs in from the right, we come to the gentle River Gowy.

The river is shallow and rimmed with bur reeds, rushes, dropwort and yellow flag iris; long fronds pushing up from the silted bottom are stroked out in the current. Though in effect still a linear nature reserve rich with wildlife, today's Gowy is a pale reminder of the ancient river.

Remember, the water level was once much higher. A wooden dugout boat, dating perhaps from the Iron Age, was found in a field near Stamford Bridge in the 1930s. But dredging at the mouth of the river and centuries of land-drainage has reduced the marshes to flat pasture. Only a few willows alongside the channels give a clue to an older landscape. Ducks and patient herons still use the river and kingfishers nest nearby, but the hosts of water birds are long gone. A last greenshank was killed at Barrowmore in 1890, and a bittern near Tarvin in 1901. Before Stanlow Oil Refinery was built in 1922, flights of noisy geese passed overhead en route to their daytime feeding grounds at dusk and dawn.

'The River Gowy has trout, pikes and eels', *noted a Cheshire naturalist in 1804. Attracted by the fish, otters could at one time be seen along the Gowy and Back Brook. Old accounts agree:* 'Otters are occasionally seen at Stamford Bridge'—*1884;* 'Three otters were seen at Stapleford'—*1892; and,* 'Five otters were ruthlessly shot and clubbed to death at Stanney'—*1902. Yet despite their welcome return to other parts of Cheshire, you are unlikely to see otters here today.*

Saint Peter's Church, Plemstall

PLEMSTALL'S ANCIENT PARISH CHURCH stands isolated among chestnuts and rare black poplars at the end of a lonely lane. Even quite recently floods have cut it off, and there is no village and only one farm to share its solitude. Why? The reason goes back over a thousand years.

Tradition says that sometime during the 7th century a shipwrecked Irish fisherman vowed that if he were saved he would build a church where he was cast ashore. He landed here, on the Isle of Chester—now 7^1/$_2$ miles/12 kilometres inland from the modern Mersey at Stanlow. In gratitude, he dedicated his church, naturally, to Peter the fisherman.

Two hundred years later, a hermit named Plegmund settled on the Isle, and the place became known as Plemstall, from *Plegmondestowe*, the fenny island of Plegmund. Plegmund preached at Chester and soon gathered a following. His fame spread, and Alfred the Great called him to his court to help reform the state. A scholar and theologian, he later became Archbishop of Canterbury, and wrote much of the famous *Anglo-Saxon Chronicles*—the earliest history of any European country in its native language.

The church was wholly rebuilt in the 15th century. The present stone tower replaced the wooden belfry only in 1826; look carefully and it's easy to trace the outline of the old church. Inside, the church is built without a separate nave and chancel, but with two adjoining naves instead. Fragments of medieval glass are preserved in the windows and the church contains a Jacobean three-decker pulpit, much rich carving and several rare Bibles.

Amongst the many old tombstones in the churchyard is the 14th century box tomb of the Hurlestons under the east window. It's carved with two skeletons (each holding the arrow of Time) one male and one female—count the ribs!

An unusual fourteenth century box tomb belonging to the Hurleston family at St Peter's Church, Plemstall

Follow the river, downstream, to the right. Before the railway embankment, turn left over a farm tractor bridge.

From its wooden sleepers look down on the lazy river, where insects and tiny fishes flicker amongst the swaying weeds.

Cross the field ahead to another stile just to the right of the outbuildings of Holme Farm.

The name Holme Farm comes from the Old English word holm, *meaning 'an islet' or 'rich, flat land beside a river'. Today the farmyard is a typical muddle of seed-trays, trailers and harrows, overlain by the sharp tang of silage and the sweet scent of cattle dung.*

Turn right, along the farm access track. Soon the thorn-edged track meets the railway line at a white, wicket gate.

Originally part of the Cheshire Lines Committee railway, trains first reached Chester on this line in 1874. Today a distant two-tone horn warns of the trains' approach, and the tracks weave and undulate away in both directions on their raised embankment across the Gowy marshes.

Cross the railway and follow the rough road to a turning area in front of St Peter's church, Plemstall.

3. From the churchyard, if you've time, make a short detour to see Plegmund's Well. Not far down the lane to Mickle Trafford and Chester is a bridge over Babbins Brook; next to it is

Framed by willows, St. Peter's Church sits above the old marshlands

Plegmund's Well. Just discernible in the surrounding stonework is the inscription:

> *'Here as in days when Alfred erst was king,*
> *Baptismal water flows from Plegmund's spring.'*

Return to the church and bear right over the cattle grid. Walk back along the farm road until the left-hand hawthorn hedge curves away to the left. Turn left, off the road and walk beside the hedge to a sturdy footbridge—with stiles at either end—that spans the Gowy. Once on the far side of the tiny river, the flatlands of the old marshes open out towards Dunham-on-the-Hill, Bridge Trafford and the Mersey.

From the bridge, cross the fields ahead, keeping the drainage ditch on your left.

Pick up a handful of the rich, dark alluvial soil. Cold winds cut across these open lands in winter; on old maps this area is aptly called the Wild Moors. Coveys of grey partridge, now declining in Cheshire, burst from beneath the feet in a flurry of wings; and long-billed snipe probe the damp soil, and then zigzag away with a call like tearing cloth.

At the top of the field is a junction of drainage ditches, crossed by another well-made footbridge. Cross the bridge and veer left, across the following field. Go over a stile and turn right along a farm track called Wildmoor Lane.

The large farm to the left, beyond Barrow Brook, is 200 acre/80 hectare Morley Hall Farm, bought for just £9,000 in 1919. The old Hall stood closer to the railway, but when the farm was burnt down the Hall was rebuilt on slightly higher ground. A Spitfire fighter-plane crashed nearby during World War Two.

Five hundred metres later, the track skirts the glasshouses and polytunnels of Barrow Nurseries who raise shrubs for the wholesale plant and landscape market: laurels, bamboos, dogwoods, cotoneasters and spiny berberis.

Beyond the nurseries, the lane meets the B5132 below the old Little Barrow station.

Look out over the fields to the left: on the horizon is the bulk of Helsby Hill from where an Iron Age hillfort dominated the heights above the Mersey and the Gowy Marshes.

4. At the road, go right, uphill, past Barrow Lodge and Little Barrow Hall.

The outbuildings of the old farm are now converted into modern homes. The mid-eighteenth century farmhouse was built from bricks made by next-door-neighbour Joseph Brock, from The Hough. Nearby was the site of Little Barrow quarry, which provided the stone for the rebuilding of Plemstall church tower in 1826. The stonemason spent the money he earned on beer and was said locally 'to have drunk Plemstall tower'!

Cross the railway bridge.

When the railway arrived in 1874 the station soon became busy. Milk was sent to Manchester at 7.30 am every morning; and two-wheeled, iron-tyred milk floats raced to the station from the outlying farms. Later in the day, trucks of coal were sometimes unloaded for the Manor House in Great Barrow. By 1945 seven trains a day passed through in each direction.' Barrow for Tarvin station', as it was called, was closed for passengers in 1953.

Beyond the bridge's high-sided parapet, the hill steepens and passes Station Farm, which was the original Little Barrow Hall. Two hundred metres later, on the left, is the Primitive Methodist Chapel, built by public subscription in 1865. For twenty years, from the 1940s, it was a shop; now it's a private house.

At the top of the hill, 300 feet/100 metres above sea level, is the Foxcote once more—a welcome end to a fascinating walk.

But before taking refreshment, look back at the spread of the old marshlands below. And picture this hilltop 5,000 years ago, when Stone-Age settlers—one of whose polished stone-axes was found nearby in 1932—first chose this sandstone outcrop as their home. Surrounded by forest and overlooking a marsh-rimmed sea bay, it must have been a far quieter, bleaker, and more isolated spot than we can properly imagine today.

3. Hockenhull Platts
Packhorse Bridges over the River Gowy

Ancient packhorse route, raised causeway across the marshes, marshy nature reserve, three medieval packhorse bridges, quiet riverside paths, old watermill, and a section of Roman Watling Street

Start: *Centre of Tarvin village, 4 miles/7 kilometres east of Chester. Map reference: SJ 490670.*

Distance: *5 miles/8 kilometres.*

Duration: *Allow 3 hours.*

Difficulty: *Virtually flat. Lanes, surfaced paths, riverside and field paths. Wet in places.*

Food and Drink: *George and Dragon, High Street, Tarvin. Real Ales. Home made food. Beer garden. 01829 741446*

Maps: *OS 1:25,000 Explorer 266 Wirral and Chester/Caer, and 267 Northwich and Delamere Forest; OS 1:50,000 Landranger 117 Chester.*

IT IS HARD TO BELIEVE, but for almost 1,400 years after the Romans left Britain in around AD410, no proper new roads were built. The Roman roads, themselves often based on earlier tracks, continued in use throughout the Middle Ages; but outside the towns they were often 'miry ways', especially in winter.

By the eighteenth century the roads were in a deplorable condition. The old system of each parish being responsible for the repair of the roads within its boundaries had broken down. Deep ruts and floods made the roads difficult and dangerous to traverse; and there are accounts of people being drowned in the potholes. Defoe in his 1724 book *Tour through Great Britain*, states that many roads had become impassable. This, he adds,

'Necessarily brought the Country to apply to Parliament; and the consequence has been that Turnpikes or Toll-bars have been set up on the several great Roads of England. Carriages, Droves of Cattle, and Travellers on Horseback are oblig'd to pay an easy Toll, which bears no comparison with the Benefit reap'd thereby'.

Paid for by the tolls, the new roads were a godsend. But when the new turnpike road from Chester to Nantwich was built in 1743, it bypassed sections of the old London-Holyhead road that had been in use for centuries. Part of this 'lost' road still exists, from Christleton, east of Chester, to Duddon, near Tarporley. It's one of the most interesting sections of medieval roadway left in this country, and certainly the best in Cheshire.

The walk

The walk begins in the centre of the quiet Cheshire village of Tarvin.

1. Walk west along the 'High Street' towards Chester.

Much of Tarvin was razed to the ground by fire in 1752; and the resultant rebuilding has given the village several splendid Georgian buildings, including the spacious George and Dragon pub. The grand Georgian house facing the end of the High Street is Tarvin Hall, built, according to a handwritten note on a Victorian photograph, in 1776.

Two hundred metres later, turn left into 'Hockenhull Lane' and continue through the housing estate for around ¼ mile/500 metres. When the road bends to the right, continue straight ahead on 'Hockenhull Lane'—now signed as a dead end.

A Roman, decorated lead spindle whorl was discovered in Hockenhull Avenue, on the east side of Hockenhull Lane, in 1952.

Carefully cross the busy A51 Tarvin bypass to the lane directly ahead. For a while, the route joins a section of the long distance Baker Way. When the lane turns right towards Hockenhull Hall, some 350 metres later, continue straight ahead to join an enclosed pathway between fields.

2. When the path meets a T-junction with another rough unsurfaced track, turn right, onto ancient Platts Lane.

That this was the old London to Holyhead road is confirmed by Ogilby's 1675 Britannia Roadbook, *which shows the route and mentions the hangman's gibbet that once stood at nearby Brown Heath, a mile/1.5 kilometres to the west. The existence of an alternative cart-road to the south—known today as the 'Egg Bridge' route—marked on the map between Boughton and Dutton Hall, suggests that Platts Lane was old even then.*

All sorts of people once came this way, strangers as well as locals. When Celia Fiennes, a Cromwellian colonel's daughter, travelled from Chester to Nantwich during her 'Grand Tour', in 1698, she wrote: 'This is a pretty rich land; you must travel on a causey [causeway] through much wood.' *And, later, she tells how* 'I was engaged by some Highway men; two fellows all of a suddain fell into the road, they look'd truss'd up with great coates and as it were bundles about them which I believe were pistols.'

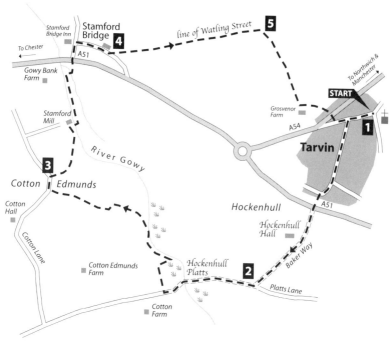

Pennant, another inveterate traveller, in his book Journey from Chester to London, *published in 1780, also mentions the 'horse road' from Christleton, across Brown Heath, to Hockenhull and Tarvin.*

While Adam Watkin, in his Observations, *published in 1791, says that* 'For many ages and to the middle of this *[the 18th]* century, a causeway about two feet wide with round pebbles was all that man or horse could travel upon... in Cheshire.'

The track winds its way down to the River Gowy.

In the past this area was a broad, reedy marshland; but now the land is drained and the river contained within high banks.

Traces of the old sandstone causeway's edges appear occasionally beside the path. Hazel bushes and dog's mercury in the deep ditch to the left suggest the hedgerow's long history; they are accepted ecological

Two of the three late eighteenth century packhorse bridges at Hockenhull Platts, near Tarvin

Hockenhull Platts Packhorse Bridges

THE THREE PACKHORSE BRIDGES, sometimes romantically known as the Roman Bridges, were probably built in their present form in the early 14th century. Records show that when the Black Prince passed over them in 1353 he ordered 20 shillings be spent on their repair. The current sandstone bridges, however, date from the late 18th century.

The sandstone bridges are joined by causeways, and are as much as 50 metres apart. Each bridge is less than 4 feet/ 1.5 metres wide and its parapet is a low 2' 6'/1 metre, while the bridge surface is of mixed cobbles and setts. Some of these are new, but many of the larger stones have evidently been worn smooth by the passage of thousands of hooves and feet, and are old.

The bridges came close to destruction in 1824 when the County Council proposed re-routeing the Nantwich to Chester road along Platts Lane. They were saved only the intercession of the Duke of Westminster, on whose land they lay.

Traces of a rectangular mound and ring ditch can be seen in low sun immediately to the south of the central arch; known simply as Hockenhull Platt earthworks, they are probably of post medieval date.

indicators of uninterrupted woodland edge habitat. In places the lane is so worn down—6-12 feet/2-4 metre below the surrounding fields— hat it becomes almost a tunnel beneath its blackthorn hedges; and we can imagine trains of packhorses slipping on the rain-wet stones during a winter descent to the Platts.

A sandstone edged causeway carries the track above the surrounding damp ground. It was once necessary, to raise the road above the Gowy marshes. In winter, the low-lying land along the Gowy is still liable to flooding. During its winding 24 mile/38 kilometres course, the Gowy falls only about 280 feet/90 metres; little enough for a river. From its mouth, where it drains into the Mersey, broad marshes once cut inland past Ince (from the Welsh ynys *meaning 'island'), Plemstall and Stamford Bridge, as far as Huxley, below the sandstone hills. And so the route to Chester had to be raised above the maze of water, rush and swamp, where sheep now graze.*

This is Hockenhull Platts.

The name is old. Its roots are Welsh—from the time when the Gowy was still called the Tarvin River, from the Welsh terfyn *meaning boundary: that is, on the Welsh border or marches.*

Similarly, the name element 'hock' may come from the Welsh hocan *meaning to peddle or sell abroad. Similarly,* hen *is the Welsh for 'old'. And* heol *means 'paved way' or road. While* platts *is an old English word for 'bridges'; a word associated with planks. So the name Hockenhull Platts is a curious amalgam of Old English and Celtic Welsh and means something like 'the bridges on the old peddlars way'.*

That the origins of the name date from a period when the Welsh-English boundary was still in what is now Cheshire, back in Anglo-Saxon times, suggests the antiquity of the road itself. It may well pre-date the medieval packhorse bridges by many centuries.

It's a peaceful spot. Dun cattle chew the cud among the aptly named 'Platt Meadows' downstream, while what in the 1860s were 'Home Croft' and 'Well Meadow' is now the 'Cheshire Wildlife Trust Hockenhull Platts Nature Reserve. Access By Permit Only'. Barn owls nest nearby and may occasionally be seen quartering the marshy fields at dusk.

But much has changed. Beneath the central bridge the arch footings are raised on an ugly concrete pontoon: the result of a scheme to lower the water level of the whole Gowy, in order to preserve Stanlow oil refinery from flooding. That's progress. Not only have the marshes vanished, but so has a complete habitat that was the haunt of otters as late as the 1880s.

Back in the 17th century Hockenhull Platts was a far wilder place, even if it was on the main road. To stop the surface degenerating into mire in winter, carts were prevented from using the road by posts set across it at intervals.

Macauley, the famous historian, writing of England in 1685, tells us how instead... 'Goods were carried by long trains of packhorses. These strong and patient beasts... were attended by a class of men who seem to have born much resemblance to the Spanish muleteers.' *The packhorses travelled in convoys of forty or more animals, with the head of each tied to the tail of the one in front. Each convoy was in charge of a* Jagger, *or driver, who walked in the lead.*

In Cheshire, one of the main commodities carried was salt from the Cheshire 'wiches': Northwich, Middlewich and Nantwich, where the natural brine springs have been exploited since prehistoric and Roman times.

Cross the old sandstone packhorse bridges. When the old track emerges between posts onto a tarmaced lane rising away from the Gowy, turn right, over a stile. A small map here shows a permissive footpath created under the Countryside Stewardship Scheme that runs alongside the Gowy before heading west across the fields to join Cotton Lane.

Follow the fence alongside the plantation beside the first field to a stile in the top right-hand corner. Then turn right, over a stile, to rejoin the River Gowy. Turn left at the river and follow the bank downstream. A hundred metres beyond a right-hand bend in the river, veer left and trace the field boundary towards another stile in the far fenceline, 50 metres or so from the corner of the field.

Cross the next small field to a footbridge across a ditch. Turn right, along the hedge, and climb over another stile. Head straight across the next field to a stile beside a gate; then skirt the margins of another large field. Towards the far side, head for a stile beside a gate that opens onto Cotton Lane. Once over the stile, turn right along Cotton Lane.

3. Roughly 150 metres later, look for a signposted footpath leading out across the fields. The path crosses the centre of the field, and then kinks left at the fence immediately before a ditch. Now head towards the farm at Stamford Mill, at the end of Mill Lane.

Cross a footbridge over a drainage ditch and head towards

the farm, aiming for a gate to the left of the house and outbuildings. Once through the gate, turn right, and pass through the farmyard. Beyond the farmhouse, the path crosses the narrow River Gowy on another bridge.

This is the site of Stamford Mill, first mentioned in documents in 1188 as molendinum de Staneford, *and referred to again in both 14th and 16th century records. A painting of 1892 shows the mill had an enclosed undershot wheel; but the wheel and its machinery were removed around 1900 when the mill was turned into a house. When the building was refurbished in 1965, two date stones from 1610 and 1790 were discovered beneath the cement render. Today, the old mill pool still stretches, broad and straight, upstream for some distance from the mill.*

Turn left immediately after the bridge and follow the path beside the river. Another access lane to the mill from Stamford Bridge once ran parallel to the path. Within 150 metres of the busy A51 ahead, turn right across a field, and take a footbridge over the ditch. Turn left and cross a second footbridge to the road.

Some 2,000 years ago the Roman road crossed the river Gowy at Stamford Bridge. The name Stamford is derived from two words: stane *and* ford, *and means the 'stony ford' or 'stone-paved ford'. Traces of the Roman road's embankment on either side of the Gowy confirm the exact crossing spot; and by 1190 old documents referring to the* pons de Stanford *suggest the ford had been replaced by a bridge by Norman times. Interestingly, a decorated Roman bronze horse bell was discovered nearby in 1956.*

Take great care crossing the busy main road, and then turn left, up the road opposite, towards Great Barrow. Nearby is the Stamford Bridge Inn—a good place for a thirst-quenching break or even lunch.

The main A51 road between Chester and here closely follows the line of Watling Street—the main Roman military road from the important legionary fortress at Chester (Deva) *to Northwich* (Condate) *and Manchester* (Mamucium). *For many centuries after the Romans left Britain, into the Middle Ages and beyond, the old Roman road continued in use as one of the major saltways radiating out from the Cheshire salt towns, or 'wiches', into Derbyshire and Wales.*

4. Opposite the Stamford Bridge Inn, turn right into a redundant loop of the old Chester-Manchester highway, now called Lansdowne Road. Beyond the houses, take the signed footpath on the left.

For the next ¹/₂ mile/1 kilometre or so, the footpath traces the route of the Roman road as it runs on across the modern fields towards Kelsall hill, Organsdale field, Eddisbury hillfort, and Oakmere to the Roman station at Northwich *(Condate)*.

Keep to the left-hand edge of the field to cross a footbridge in the far corner. Cross another small field and a second footbridge, and continue along the left-hand hedgeline.

Continue through the fields ahead.

5. When the path meets a footbridge on the left, about ³/₄ mile/ 1 kilometre from Lansdowne Road, veer right, across the fields towards Tarvin. Although the Roman road runs on, gently uphill towards Kelsall, we turn aside onto the old footpath used for centuries by local people taking the shortest walking route between Great Barrow and Tarvin.

Soon Tarvin church comes into view. Cross the stile and footbridge in the field corner and continue alongside the hedge. Just before farm buildings, turn left over a footbridge and keep to the field boundary on the right. A gate on the right leads out onto the A54. Cross the main road with care and walk along the short road opposite. At the T-junction, turn left and walk back into the centre of Tarvin village to complete the walk.

4. Shocklach

Around Castletown

Isolated Norman church, ancient cross, ghostly procession, shifting river, medieval lanes, Norman castle mound and ditches, Roman road, lost medieval settlement

---

Start: *Shocklach, 2¹/₂ miles/4 kilometres south of Farndon. Map Reference: SJ 432502.*

Distance: *2 miles/3 kilometres.*

Duration: *Allow 2-2¹/₂ hours.*

Difficulty: *Mostly flat, green lanes, field paths and farm tracks. Muddy in winter. Not suitable for pushchairs.*

Food and Drink: *The Bull Inn Country Bistro, Parr Green Lane, Shocklach. Freehouse. Bar snacks and evening meals. Children welcome. 01829 250239.*

Maps: *OS 1:25,000 Explorer 257 Crewe and Nantwich; OS 1:50,000 Landranger 117 Chester, Wrexham and surrounding area.*

THE WELSH-ENGLISH BORDER has shifted to and fro over the centuries. Today the line follows the natural boundary of the River Dee for a while between Aldford and Shocklach; on the one side is Cheshire, and on the other Wrexham County Borough, in the North Wales Borderlands. But frontiers aren't immutable; they move. Until the seventh century, Cheshire was under Celtic, Welsh control. Just a hundred years later, Anglian settlers from north Germany had pushed the Welsh back into the hills. And by the tenth century the Anglian kingdom of Mercia was 'shired', or sheared, off and became a separate Shire, a forerunner of the Norman county of Cheshire.

Both Wat's Dyke and Offa's Dyke mark the changing fortunes of the Mercian marches, or borders, west of the Dee, in what is now Wales. While to the east, in Cheshire, the name Tarvin points to an earlier Celtic line—in Welsh *terfyn* means boundary; in those days, the tiny River Gowy marked the frontier.

From then on, through Norman times and later, the often marshy land on either side of the Dee was bandit country. Two Welshmen thought to be outlaws were captured at Shocklach in 1387 by the Constable of Holt and 28 armed men. The border was a no-man's-land of castles, cattle raids and uncertainty. If it seems peaceful today, in the past the silence could be misleading, the lull before the storm.

The walk

The walk begins a mile/1.5 kilometres north of the tiny village of Shocklach, 11 miles/18 kilometres south of Chester. From Farndon towards Shocklach, an unclassified road winds south, parallel to the Dee. Some 350 metres beyond a roadside sign announcing the village of Shocklach is an unmarked single-track lane leading down to the river; only an obscure wooden sign simply marked 'Church' suggests that it leads anywhere.

The lane slopes gently down towards the river with the panorama of the Welsh hills spread out in front.

1. Park at the bottom of the lane, close to the bend. There is a gravelled parking area for churchgoers in a field beside the church.

Hidden among shadowed conifers and horse chestnuts here is the little known Norman church of St. Edith's, Shocklach. But first, take a look at the nearby, recently restored brick building; it's a tiny stable, built only 50 years after the end of the Civil War, where the curate and the better-off members of his congregation left their horses during services. Unpeg the stable door and look inside, through an iron grille. Notes on the end wall outside explain the history of the church and tell us 'Mrs Hebblewhite, born in Milton House, Shocklach, clearly remembers two horses being stabled here—Moses and Aaron— and a pony, Nell.' *Curiously, the stable once boasted a fireplace, a coal shed, and an outside privy.*

The church's odd position, away from any farms, houses or other habitations is the result of the plague. Some time in the Middle Ages, frightened villagers moved their homes away from the church, to avoid the 'pestilential airs' rising from the churchyard. Ever since, the church has sat out in the fields, like some social outcast. Later, we'll pass the site of the medieval settlement, now sinking back into the landscape.

Enter the churchyard through the wooden gate.

Tall Victorian tombstones mingle with solid box tombs, most with dates from the 1800s; but half hidden in the turf below the east window is a recumbent slab with the barely visible date of 1664. At the turn of the last century the old custom of strewing the graves with rushes at certain times of year was still observed at this out of the way place.

Opposite the beautifully carved Norman doorway, is an ancient octagonal cross shaft remounted on a later plinth. Still in its original position on the south side of the church, the cross has a significant history. Church crosses were where labourers were hired each year by the local farmers, where payments were made, where pedlars sold their wares, and where parish matters were settled.

Shocklach cross was also used as a plague stone. Epidemics swept Cheshire several times in the 16th- and 17th centuries and, even in this quiet corner, families and whole communities were devastated. But life must go on; and in around 1600 the cross shaft was used as a market place. Look on the top: the four fist-sized depressions in the stone were once filled with vinegar to disinfect coins; food and other necessities of life were left nearby, and business was conducted at what they hoped was a safe distance.

If you wish to look inside the church, a note beside the main door tells us: 'This church is open for quiet prayer 10.00-11.00 Wednesday mornings.'

Leaving the church, go out into the lane through the wooden kissing gate. Turn left and left again as the grassy track runs on down towards the river and the old crossing place. Referred to in early documents, this was the main road from Castletown to Wrexham in medieval times.

Local legend also says this green lane is the scene of an occasional

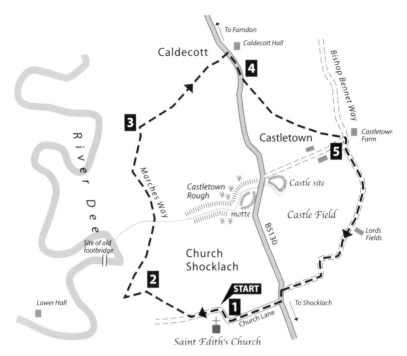

haunting. For, so the story goes, the Breretons, Barons of Malpas, some on horseback and some in coaches, come this way in the darkness in a long and opulent procession to view their old domain. And at midnight the ghostly family halts and climbs down to visit their remote and isolated church.

Ignore the first stile that climbs into the field to the right, still opposite the church. Instead, walk on down the lane and go over a second stile on the right, beside a metal field gate 150 metres on. Head diagonally across the large sloping field for a stile almost in the far corner.

2. Once in the next field, our route must follow the public right of way in a sharp dogleg that doubles back to another stile in the same hedgeline less than 100 metres to the right. A quick look at the map shows the distinct 'V'-shape taken by the paths. If only we could take a short cut!

But, keeping to the footpath, veer left across the field and cross

Saint Edith's Church, Shocklach

SAINT EDITH'S CHURCH, SHOCKLACH, is said to be the oldest Cheshire church that still holds weekly services. It was built in about 1150 by the lord of the manor, Thomas de Shocklach (who lived in the nearby Norman castle), to serve the three townships of Caldecott, Church Shocklach and Shocklach Oviatt. However, the fact that it is dedicated to St. Edith of Polesworth, one of the sisters of the Saxon King Edward the Elder suggest there was probably an earlier Saxon church here long before the Norman conquest. The church's curious position may also mark an ancient crossing point on the Dee—a ford or ferry—where travellers could stop to pray before they crossed or give thanks afterwards.

Many maps fail to show the Grade I listed church; and looking at them one can only surmise the church's position by the meeting of ancient tracks and paths.

'*Socheliche*' is how the name appears in the Domesday Book. '*Lache*' meant mire or slutch. So Shocklach comes out as just another muddy-sounding form of 'such slutch', or something close. An indication of the church's long isolation is scratched with a diamond ring upon the east window, by travellers taking sanctuary overnight: '*I Robt. Aldersley was here the 31st day of October 1756 along with John Massie and Mr Derbyshire. NB. The roads were so bad we were in danger of our lives.*'

The church is small and simple. The only exterior refinement is the fine Norman south doorway, with its typical round-headed entrance carved with chevrons (zig-zags) and rope-like cables. The double bell cote houses a pair of bells which were originally rung from outside.

Inside the church are a 15th century font, 18th century altar rails, and two Elizabethan sanctuary chairs. Carved into the stone in the northwest corner, is a recently rediscovered relief of a mounted medieval knight in armour.

The Norman doorway and cross at St Edith's Church, Shocklach

the deep midfield drainage ditch on a low, stone tractor bridge close to the left-hand hedge. Follow the field boundary for 100 metres to another stile beneath gnarled oak and ash trees. A waymarker for the 'Marches Way' points back to the right.

Huge water-worn branches and tree trunks dot the pasture, left high and dry by winter floods. The three deep crescent-shaped gulleys here are the remains of successive ox-bow loops of the old river—long since cut off and silted up. Now solid and overgrown, they lead to the water's edge. The Dee is still scouring at its sandy banks, cutting out yet another future loop. A map of 1874 shows an island close by. A little upstream there used to be a footbridge that crossed over into Wales; and, until the 1950s, there was a Ferry Cottage too.

Head diagonally upslope across the rough pasture. Recross the drainage ditch (!) and climb over a stile in the hedge at the top of the field. It's waymarked for the 'Marches Way'. Warmer and perhaps wetter, you're back on the same hedge that the path left a while ago.

Once over the stile, veer left, out across the sloping pasture to another waymarked stile in the hedgeline below Castletown Rough.

Go straight across this smaller field, keeping the hedge on your right, and climb over another stile in the top, right-hand corner. A narrow plank bridge traverses a ditch beneath a field maple tree.

Now turn left, and head for an unmarked gap in the hedge less than 50 metres away. Cross the next field, and within 100 metres, climb over another combined short plank bridge and stile through a gap in the hedge.

Still on the 'Marches Way', veer uphill to the right and away from the river, passing a pond on your left where herons and moorhens feed.

The many small ponds that spangle Cheshire's farmland—look at the 1:25,000 Explorer maps—are marl pits where in the past specialist contractors dug out marl, a limey glacial clay once used as a kind of primitive fertiliser. Now they are havens for wildlife; and cattle drink at their rush-choked rims.

A hundred metres beyond the pond, cross a waymarked stile in the hedgerow.

3. Within 20 metres, turn right, through a broad gateway. Our route leaves the 'Marches Way' here and heads, instead, back towards Caldecott Hall on the Farndon-Shocklach road. Cross the field to the gate on the far side. Then follow the broad farm lane until it meets the Farndon-Shocklach road.

Keeping an eye out for traffic, turn right, along the road towards Castletown.

4. When the road bends to the right, less than 200 metres later, go through the field gate in the hedge on the left. The public right of way heads out across the field to the right, towards a distant house fringed by tall pines at Castletown.

Over a stile the path bends to the left. Keep to the left of two old marl pits, and head for a field gate in the far hedgeline. Go over the waymarked stile beside the gate, veer to the right and head for the far right-hand corner of the field by Castletown Farm.

5. Over the stile, turn right on an ancient green lane.

Broad and grassy, the lane is now part of Bishop Bennet's Way—a 55 kilometre/34 mile long distance route for walkers, horse riders and mountain bikers that traces bridleways, byways and minor roads between Beeston Castle and Wirswall, near Whitchurch. The Way is named after Bishop Bennet, a Georgian churchman, antiquarian and member of the House of Lords who traced the route of many old roads across Cheshire in the 1790s and early 1800s.

The green lane is a section of the old Roman road that ran south from Chester (Deva) *to Wroxeter* (Viroconium), *south of Shrewsbury. Leaving Chester via modern Handbridge and Eccleston, the road forded the Dee at Aldford (old ford), passing to the east of Farndon and Churton before heading south-east to Castletown. Much of the route can be traced on the map as surviving lanes, tracks and bridleways today.*

By the late Norman period, the road had been adopted and the name changed to King's Street. In places the route had changed slightly to avoid muddy sections of the by then ancient and decaying Roman road.

On the opposite side of the old road, in the two large fields immediately to the left and right of Castletown Farm, are the mounds and hollows of the lost medieval settlement of Castletown. These are the raised house platforms or **tofts**, *and their small enclosures or* **crofts**. *In the fields to the east are the well-preserved medieval cultivation strips known as* **ridge** and **furrow**. *The settlement was associated with Shocklach's* **motte** and **bailey** *castle and the later moated manor house nearby.*

The village was moved here away from the potentially plague infected burial ground at St Edith's church. Today the various parts of the Castletown site are Scheduled Monuments, and legally protected against ploughing, cultivation or other disturbance to retain the underlying archaeology for future generations.

Soon the green lane merges with the tarmaced farm road. For the next 200 metres the lane traces the route of the Roman road

The early Norman castle mound, or motte, *beside the entrance to Castletown Farm, at Shocklach*

before curving to the right. In the past, the Roman road carried on, straight ahead, across the fields towards Wroxeter.

The modern farm lane snakes through rich Cheshire farmland, past Lordsfields Farm, and back to the Farndon-Shocklach road. At the end of Castsletown Lane, a black and white cast-iron signpost points back to 'Castletown ¹/₂' and left to 'Shocklach'.

Away to the right is the site of the Norman castle from which Castletown takes its name. It's a short detour of less than 500 metres each way along the road to the right, towards Farndon; but if you choose to walk, take care of speeding traffic on the narrow road. Otherwise, turn left, towards Shocklach.

Immediately before the entrance to Castletown House Farm (see the map), look over the fence to the right.

Here, and deep in the woods opposite, are the still impressive remains of an early Norman castle. Following their conquest of Britain, the Normans built scores of minor strongholds across the country to consolidate local control. Hugh Lupus (the wolf!), Earl of Chester and nephew to William the Conqueror, established a line of castles southwest of Chester at Dodleston, Pulford, Aldford, Shocklach, Oldcastle, and Newhall near Combermere. Those at Aldford and Shocklach guarded ancient crossing points on the river Dee. Their common purpose was to protect Chester's vulnerable flank down the Welsh border.

Wood and earth were the materials most easily to hand, and the castles were of the motte and bailey *type, similar to those shown on the Bayeux Tapestry. The* motte *was a high mound of earth with a palisade around the top, and the* bailey *was a courtyard protected by another palisade and ditch.*

At Castletown, even 800 years after they were built, the Norman ramparts still stand some four metres/12 feet above the surrounding fields. Ormerod, the Victorian Cheshire historian, writing in the 1840s tells us the mound was then, ' ... circular, and about twenty feet in perpendicular height'. *Though dry today, the moat was originally fed by the stream that snakes across Castle Field. Imagine the castle as it must once have looked, a statement of Norman power; a fortress in the wilderness.*

Having completed, or to omit, this detour, turn left along the road towards Shocklach. Within 30 metres, turn right, back down narrow, metalled Church Lane as it slopes towards secluded St Edith's church, the river Dee, and the end of the walk.

5. Willington

Above 'Little Switzerland'

Hidden valley, shelf-like path, Iron Age hillfort, Ice Age meltwater gorge, and pleasant views

Start: *Sandstone Trail car park, Willington Corner, 1 mile/0.5 kilometre southeast of Kelsall. Map reference: SJ 534667.*

Distance: *3 miles/5 kilometres.*

Duration: *Allow 2 hours.*

Difficulty: *Gentle ascent to the top of Boothsdale. Quiet lanes, sandy footpaths, forest tracks and field paths. Mostly dry.*

Food and Drink: *The Boot Inn, Boothsdale, Willington. Open every lunchtime and evenings. Bar snacks. Restaurant. Beer garden. Children welcome during meal times. 01829 751375. OR Summertrees Tearoom and Garden, Tirley Lane, Willington. Home made hot and cold food, teas, sandwiches, baked potatoes. Open every day except Fridays. Children, muddy boots, and dogs welcome. 01829 751145.*

Maps: *OS 1:25,000 Explorer 267 Northwich and Delamere Forest; OS 1:50,000 Landranger 117 Chester & Wrexham.*

'WILLINGTON', SO KELLY'S DIRECTORY OF CHESHIRE for 1912 tells us, '*is a parish 3½ miles south from Mouldsworth Station...*'. At first glance, this seems an odd way to start a summary of a place. But there is a good reason. When the Cheshire Lines railway from Manchester to Chester opened in the 1840s, the city's crowded workers were keen to escape into the countryside on the train— for affordable cars had yet to come—and Willington seized its opportunity. Until the First World War, Willington was known as 'Little Switzerland'; and the first 'tourists' came to stay in local cottages, to climb the hills, to walk in the quiet lanes and to take a breath of Cheshire air. Looking back from an age of cheap flights and package holidays it seems a quaint idea; but then much has changed since then—in both Willington and the world.

The walk

The walk around 'Little Switzerland' begins in the quiet foothills settlement of Willington.

Turn off the A54 Kelsall bypass at the top of the hill, and drop down through the now peaceful village on the old main road. Turn left at the footbridge, on the signposted road to Willington, and turn left again into Willington Lane. Half-a-mile/1 kilometre along Willington Lane, turn left into Chapel Lane, at Willington Corner, and pull into the parking area for the Sandstone Trail. Three bays beneath the trees provide parking for up to 20 cars.

1. Turn right out of the car park and walk uphill on Chapel Lane.

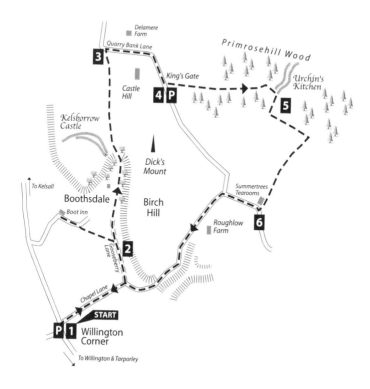

Towards the top of Chapel Lane, look for market gardens hidden by tall hedges. Fruit has been grown at Willington since at least the 1940s. Clever positioning on the slopes of Willington Hill ensure the fruit is above the early and late frost levels, while shelter belts of tall conifers protect the vulnerable buds and flowers from the prevailing westerly winds. Apples, strawberries, blackcurrants, rhubarb, broad and runner beans and other vegetables thrive in the rich soil, with traditional Cheshire damsons in the hedgerows. Perhaps the best known of the local fruit farms is Winsors, whose Farm Shop at the top of Chapel Lane sells a range of fruits in season as well as other local and home made produce.

Where the road forks at the top of Chapel Lane, turn left into Gooseberry Lane.

Strangely, the name is older than the fruit farms, which were started only after World War Two; and its origin is obscure. What were once small, rural workers' cottages hug the slope; all have now been enlarged

The unique hanging path that ascends the side of Boothsdale

beyond recognition. As the lane ascends, the view opens out to the left, and the name 'Little Switzerland' takes on a clearer meaning. If large-eyed dun cows with bells around their necks ambled across flower-spangled meadows, it wouldn't seem surprising.

Many of the cottages perched on the steep bank date from the 1860s; and even in 1911, the population of Willington as a whole was still only 139. Even so, the cottagers were quick to seize the opportunity of a second income and, according to the oldest resident of Gooseberry Lane in the 1990s, 'the cottages would clear a bedroom out', *and offer bed and breakfast to visitors who arrived from the station in horse-drawn carts. Later, a van came out twice a week from Nantwich to supply local people with groceries.*

2. Ignore a signposted footpath on the left—which leads downhill to the Boot Inn at the bottom of Boothsdale—and carry on along Gooseberry Lane. When the lane peters out towards the last house high on the bank, continue on the gravelled track ahead.

Soon a concrete drive rises to the right; go straight ahead here on a narrow, waymarked footpath between the house and the lower part of the garden.

This curious raised path runs through a green tunnel that hugs the wooded slopes. Below, to the left, is the hidden combe of Boothsdale. The path's age is uncertain but the drystone walls on either side—one dropping away, and the other holding back the hillside—make it perhaps unique in Cheshire. Green flowered pennywort, wood sage, and the spires of purple foxgloves decorate the crevices. And, where the sweeping branches of horse chestnuts arch over the path, it's like being on a natural veranda, perched high above the valley.

Beyond a flight of timber-edged steps, close to the top, stop on the bend and look back.

Photogenically framed by trees, Boothsdale opens out below. The view has changed little since the first visitors from industrial Manchester gazed out over the Cheshire Plain from here a generation or more ago. In the foreground, a handful of typical Cheshire cottages shelter in the hollow. The dark shelterbelts of tall conifers are relatively new, but the green chequer-board of small fields beyond would be familiar to anyone standing here at the turn of the last century. The

Peckforton and Bickerton hills stretch away to the left, with the outlying wedge of Harthill jutting out towards Wales. Closer to the Dee you can see the tall bell tower of Eaton Hall—the home of the Duke of Westminster—once a Victorian palace, but since replaced by a modern monstrosity and, according to an elderly Willington resident, 'all lights now'.

Beyond a second flight of steps, at the top of the path, climb over a stile, out of the trees and into open pasture.

It's a different world. The remaining sturdy three-barred fences here are a reminder of the days when Castle Hill was a stud farm for prize shire horses. For a fee of between three pounds ten shillings and six guineas, the stallions were taken out to sire foals as far away as Chester, Helsby, and the Wirral.

During the Second World War, the RAF communications aerial, up on Dick's Mount to the right here, meant local people had to be especially vigilant over the black out; a light here could be seen from Wales and, for fear of being bombed or strafed, 'you mustn't even strike a match'.

A standing stone in the fields here, known as the 'Whipping Stone', was removed in the 19th century. Local consensus suggests it wasn't prehistoric but instead marked the site of a prize stallion's grave. In contrast, the encircling prehistoric bank and ditch of Kelsborrow Castle are clearly visible in the pastures ahead.

The path bears right and continues alongside the fence towards Castle Hill Farm. Go over two stiles to a metal kissing gate beneath the trees. Beyond a narrow strip of woodland, the path crosses a tarmac drive to emerge on Quarry Bank Lane.

3. Turn right and follow the lane gently uphill as it bends to the right past Delamere Farm and Sandstone House.

Over the crest of the hill, 150 metres on, turn left into Primrosehill Wood, at King's Gate.

4. A wooden signpost at the rear of the parking area points to the Sandstone Trail. Follow the limestone-surfaced track downhill into the woods. Continue past a signed path off to the left to 'Nettleford Wood'. At the bottom of the slope, the path joins the Sandstone Trail. Another signpost points left to 'Delamere' and

Kelsborrow Castle

AN OVAL IRON AGE PROMONTORY-FORT, Kelsborrow Castle takes advantage of the natural headland created by Boothsdale on the southeast and the steep scarp across the fields to the west. Although there is higher ground to the east, the 400-feet/125 metres high site would be easy to defend. Centuries of ploughing have spread the soil of the ramparts that curve around the north side of the 7-acre/3 hectare enclosure. Even so, the earthwork banks still rise at least 6 feet/2 metres above the bottom of the outer ditch. The defences were formidable, and were almost certainly once topped by a wooden palisade. No doubt they protected a settlement of round houses with conical thatched roofs. There is no sign of the fort's entrance along the rampart, and it seems probable that, as elsewhere, access was along the edge of the slope, close to the path up from Boothsdale.

Kelsborrow was the home of people of the peace-loving *Cornovii* tribe, who were later easily subdued by the Romans. Traces of small Celtic fields have been found to the north, in Kelsall, while the area carries numerous clues, in the form of Neolithic flint tools, to long occupation by people well before the Iron Age.

Although Kelsborrow Castle has yet to be excavated, a 6 inch/15 centimetre bronze axe-head was found nearby in 1810 and, later, a section of an iron sword. Kelsborrow Castle is a protected Scheduled Monument on private ground.

right to 'Beeston Castle'. Follow the broad, limestone-surfaced track around to the right.

At the bottom of the dip, 50 metres on, the Sandstone Trail turns sharply to the right at another signpost for 'Summertrees and Beeston Castle'. Directly opposite this junction, a narrow woodland path heads into the trees. It's worth making a brief detour here to visit mysterious Urchin's Kitchen.

Walk away from the Sandstone Trail and into the woods.

Old postcard of 'Little Switzerland', Boothsdale, Willington. around 1910

Within 50 metres, the path descends into an atmospheric sandstone gorge overhung by Scots pines and scrubby rhododendrons.

This is Urchin's Kitchen. It's one of several glacial drainage channels in the area formed beneath a vast lowland ice sheet at the close of the last Ice Age; there are others nearby at Hollins Gutter and Dogfall. As the climate warmed and the ice sheet retreated northwards, glacial meltwater under immense pressure eroded these gullies along natural faults in the underlying Triassic sandstone. As the path descends into the water-worn gorge, the sandstone sides are exposed. Careful inspection of the different layers shows how these so-called Helsby Sandstones were laid down by braided rivers in a desert landscape. In the lower beds, the river currents ran southwards, while the upper beds show a north to north-westerly flow—the more usual direction in Cheshire.

The curious name Urchin's Kitchen may derive from an old country name for hedgehogs. Perhaps this sheltered gorge with its drifts of autumn leaves was once a favourite place for hibernating hedgehogs?

5. From Urchin's Kitchen, return to the main Sandstone Trail and go straight ahead on the narrow, sandy section of the Trail signposted to 'Summertrees and Beeston'. At the fenceline, 50 metres later, turn left and continue uphill on the waymarked Sandstone Trail. The path climbs gently with open pastures on the right. Close to the top of the slope, look out for another waymarker post on the left. Turn right here, up a short flight of steps and through a metal kissing gate beneath tall sycamore trees.

Out in open farmland now, the path follows the field edge uphill. On the brow of the slope, 100 metres later, go right, through another kissing gate, and continue along the far side of the hedge to the left.

Beyond two more kissing gates, the path emerges on Tirley Lane beside Summertrees Tearoom and Garden—an attractive, family run café that welcomes walkers.

6. Turn right, past the front of Summertrees, and walk on down Tirley Lane. Bear left at the T-junction and follow Roughlow Lane downhill past Summer Bank and Roughlow Farm.

The name Roughlow suggests there may once have been a Bronze Age burial mound, tumulus, or low nearby. It's yet more evidence that the Cheshire Sandstone Ridge was home to prehistoric people at a distant time when much of lowland Cheshire was a maze of impenetrable woodland, mire and moss.

Soon the road snakes sharply downhill, cut into the contour of the hill.

Sandstone juts from the road's uphill edge, while parts of the downhill side are supported by concrete blocks put there by labour gangs of Italian prisoners of war in the 1940s. The deep combe hidden amid the trees here is called Pearl Hole, a reference to a lost water source. The name Pearl comes from the Old English word for a spring.

Past several cottages balanced on the lip of the slope, Roughlow Lane rejoins Gooseberry Lane and Chapel Lane opposite Winsor's Fruit farm. From this junction, you can either return down 'Chapel Lane' to the car park at Willington Corner, or walk up 'Gooseberry Lane' and take the footpath to the left that leads down Boothsdale to the secluded 'Boot Inn'.

6. Delamere

Along Roman Watling Street, below the Hillfort

Iron Age and Saxon hillfort, Roman roads, medieval quarry, and round the 'Old Pale'

Start: *The Sandstone Trail car park, Barnsbridge Gates, Delamere Forest Park. Map reference: SJ 542715.*

Distance: *6 miles/9.5 kilometres.*

Duration: *Allow 3-3¹/₂ hours.*

Difficulty: *Forest and undulating hills. Forestry tracks and field paths. Some slopes. Usually dry.*

Food and Drink: *Carriers Inn and Restaurant, Hatchmere Crossroads, Norley. Real ales. Food all week, lunchtimes and evenings. Beer garden. Children welcome. 01928 788258.*

Maps: *OS 1:25,000 Explorer 267 Northwich and Delamere Forest; OS 1:50,000 Landranger 117 Chester and Wrexham.*

IRON AGE CHESHIRE—in the five centuries before the Romans came —was not the untouched wilderness we might suppose. A line of hillforts along Cheshire's central sandstone ridge marked what, even then, was a far earlier trade route; one that had already seen Neolithic polished stone axes from the axe-factories of north Wales, the Lleyn peninsula and Cumbria, and gold from Ireland, pass to and fro for two thousand years. There were other routes too, from the brine springs at what are now Northwich, Middlewich and Nantwich, that crossed the Cheshire Plain from east to west. By the Iron Age both tracks were long established.

There were far fewer people then, of course. But for centuries Celtic Iron Age tribes had loved, quarrelled, eaten, slept and died in Cheshire. The *Deceangli* to the west, and the *Cornovii* to the east, were nomadic pastoralists whose flocks ranged over the drier uplands. When they settled, it was to cultivate small square fields cleared from the still extensive woodlands. And to protect themselves, during a period of climatic decline and already increasing population, they built hillforts.

Eddisbury hillfort, near Delamere, stands close to a probable prehistoric crossroads, at a meeting of two ancient tracks. It's one of history's focal points; and the theme for our walk.

The walk

The walk begins at the large Sandstone Trail car park at Barnsbridge Gates, on the Hatchmere to Ashton 'switchback' road in the heart of Delamere Forest.

1. From the far end of the car park, a small path curves out onto a broad forest track. Turn left, and head south. The track is part of the Sandstone Trail, and clearly waymarked with a black bootprint on a yellow ground. The broad, surfaced track meanders beneath tall oaks and sweet chestnuts.

Delamere Forest Park was the first Forestry Commission site in the North West to be opened up to the public as open access land under the Countryside Rights of Way Act. This gives walkers the right to roam freely in the forest in perpetuity. However, on public safety grounds, some areas may need to be legally closed for short periods while tree felling and other potentially dangerous management tasks are completed. This new freedom is of particular interest for anyone who wants to explore Eddisbury hillfort and the Old Pale, which are central to this walk.

At a major crossroads of forest tracks, go straight ahead, still on the Sandstone Trail. White routed-out lettering on a tall square wooden post points ahead to 'White Moor Trail—7 miles'.

When the limestone-surfaced forest track swings to the right, some 200 metres later, go straight ahead, on a narrower path. The path curves uphill to the left, waymarked for the 'Baker Way', before crossing a railway bridge.

Fifty metres beyond the railway bridge, go straight on a junction of paths, still on the waymarked Sandstone Trail.

2. A hundred metres later, at the top of a slight rise near

Eddisbury Lodge, the Sandstone Trail continues straight ahead: but we bear left on the waymarked 'Baker Way'.

The broad, sandy path drops into a dip beneath tall pines and crosses a stream. At the top of the slope, the path bears to the right, before recrossing the stream and curving uphill to the left.

3. When the path meets a broad, limestone-surfaced forestry track, cross over to enter the 'Old Pale Woodland'. (The track to the left goes to the Forest Enterprise Visitor Centre).

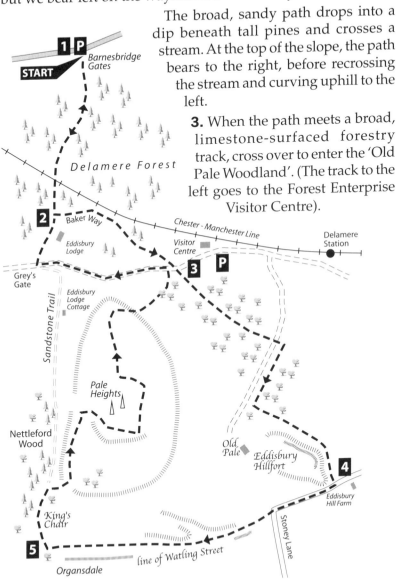

The Old Pale is former farmland. Three hundred and forty acres/ 137 hectares were bought by the Forestry Commission in December 2000 and painstakingly landscaped and planted to create different habitats. A suggestion that the area's original lowland heath could be recreated was sadly rejected and the farmland transformed instead into a mosaic of open grassland and mixed woodland. Although an inspired ecological opportunity was missed, the area is still attractive to wildlife. In particular, it's a 'butterfly hotspot'—with 15 species discovered during a brief three-day survey in 2001, and more expected over a full season. Species seen here include gatekeeper, meadow brown, small copper, small tortoiseshell, and wall brown.

Follow the broad track that runs along the bottom of the hillside, with Eddisbury Hill and Pale Heights rising above you to the right. To the left is Eddisbury Wood. Ignore occasional side paths. Roughly ¹/₂ mile/1 kilometre from the edge of the old forest, cross a narrow tarmaced road, and go through a gap in the hedge almost opposite.

Turn right on a grassy path that rises uphill between the young trees. At the top of the slope, 500 metres later, turn left across the hillside, and follow the contour along the upper edge of the new plantations.

Out to the left, the view spans the Cheshire Plain, with the Peak District hills faint on the horizon. Look out, too, for the white dish of the Joddrell Bank radio telescope in the middle distance.

Go through a gateway and continue ahead along the top edge of a second plantation. The earthen ramparts of Eddisbury hillfort rise up to the right. While the path continues around the base of the ramparts, this is open access land and you are free to climb the lower ramparts—although the hillfort itself is on private land.

From high on Eddisbury Hill—a flat-topped plateau of Keuper sandstone, covered with 2-3 feet/1 metre of glacial drift—the view encompasses the dark swathes of ancient Delamere Forest. Now clad in mixed broad-leaved and coniferous plantations, the forest was once a mosaic of open, sandy heathland and mixed oak-woodland. The forest soil is sand and gravel and, though poor, is light, well drained and easy to till.

Eddisbury is the oldest, largest and most complex of the late Bronze Age/early Iron Age hillforts along Cheshire's central sandstone ridge

This attracted Bronze Age settlers, long before the fort was built. Theirs are the seven tumuli—or burial mounds, 1 mile/1.5 kilometres southeast of Eddisbury, at Seven Lows Farm. There are many others, too, in and around the forest: Coblow, Roughlow, Oulton Low, Hounslow, Rulow, Garraslow, Kelsbarrow, Willow Wood, and Wanslow Well. Sadly, most have disappeared, ploughed out by centuries of agriculture.

Five wedge-shaped Neolithic stone hammers were found at the foot of Eddisbury Hill in 1896. And in 1851 a Bronze Age burial urn containing burnt human bones was discovered close to the Roman road, about ½ mile/1 kilometre from Eddisbury Hill Farm. According to the Victorian finder, one of the large stones covering the urn was 'like a human bust'.

The path traces the base of the hillfort's massive ramparts, narrowing close to Eddisbury Hill Farm. Beyond the hillfort, the path emerges onto Eddisbury Hill Lane, almost opposite the sandstone farmhouse.

Eddisbury Hillfort

EDDISBURY HILLFORT is the largest and most complex Iron Age site in Cheshire. It was built initially in the late Bronze Age/ early Iron Age—hundreds of years before the arrival of the Romans—to guard the route through the Kelsall Gap. It has a long history of both legendary and proved use.

When the fort was excavated by Liverpool University in 1935-38, they found two distinct prehistoric phases. Research showed that, at first, a single bank and ditch enclosed only the eastern end of the hill. Later on, the fort was enlarged to take in the whole of the hill top; an area roughly the same as the large field we see today. The first stage rampart and ditch were buried under the edges of the new defences, and were only discovered during excavation.

When the Romans arrived, they quickly overran most British hillforts using arrow-firing artillery and disciplined siege tactics. At Eddisbury, the palisades and earth ramparts were thrown down, and the ditches levelled. The Romans may have used the hill as a signal station, but otherwise Eddisbury remained a deserted ruin for the next 800 years.

Long after the Romans had left Britain, the fort was rebuilt by Aethelflaeda, the daughter of Alfred the Great in around AD915 to help protect Cheshire against the Danes. New ramparts were built over the Iron Age remains, and new ditches cut. It is these massive earthworks—which still tower 18 feet/6 metres above the silted-up ditch, that we can see today as a double line of defences to the east and north. The name Eddisbury is Anglo-Saxon and comes from *Eades' Byrig*, which means the fort belonging to Eade.

On a saucier note, according to local farm workers, the hillfort was a popular spot with courting couples during the 1950s and '60s; and doubtless some of our Cheshire born parents and grandparents were conceived here on warm summer nights.

4. Turn right, along this narrow, hilltop country lane. It crests a rise and then runs on downhill past aptly named 'Old Pale' cottages. The lane was still an unsurfaced farm track as late as the 1930s. Beyond the hedge on the right, open pasture rises to the outcropping sandstone sill that forms a natural base for part of the hillfort.

Four hundred metres later, the road bends left on Stoney Lane, once more prosaically known as Eddisbury Road, down towards the A556. Instead, continue through the field gate on the corner, straight ahead, on the signposted footpath.

We're now almost on the line of the Manchester (Mamucium) *to Chester* (Deva) *Roman road called Watling Street. From Northwich* (Condate), *to the east, the road climbed beneath the native hillfort on Eddisbury Hill, and then followed the contours along the slope of the high ground, towards Chester. In the past the lower ground downslope to the left was damper and even swampy, as the local names on old maps suggest—nearby are Plovers Moss, Thieves Moss and Riley Moss—obliging the Roman engineers to keep to the tops. From the gate, the Roman road ran some 50 metres down the hillside, parallel to our path. In Victorian times, a section of the road was discovered here in a spinney above the school; but, like many archaeological relics, it has since succumbed to modern mechanised farming.*

It's easy to forget that until the new turnpike road from Northwich to Chester was built in 1769, this was not just the old road, but also the only road. Roman roads continued in use throughout the Middle Ages. During the Jacobite Rebellion in 1745, local people dug a trench across the road near here in a vain attempt to block the southern march of Bonnie Prince Charlie's troops.

The path follows the field edge towards a group of Scots pines.

The stand of Scots pines, by the hedge 350 metres on, holds a remnant of what was described rather grandly by its discoverer as 'the most remarkable section of a Roman road in Britain.' It's just off the path. Still clear in the rough grass today is a 10 feet/3 metres deep hollow cut into a brow of the hill. Here in 1885, the Victorian author of Roman Cheshire, *W.T. Watkin, made an exploratory excavation. He found a 36 feet/11 metres wide cutting with a 10 feet/3 metres wide*

The Victorian excavation of Roman Watling Street in Organsdale Field, in 1885

roadway in the middle. Worn 10 inches/25 centimetres into the rock were the wheel ruts of carts; exactly 4½ feet/1.5 metres apart, they were identical in gauge to those on the well-known section of Roman road over Blackstone Edge, east of Manchester.

A hundred metres on, beyond a field gate, the route of the Roman road follows the hedge-line for a while, beneath a clump of oaks and Scots pines.

As the dotted line on the Ordnance Survey Explorer map shows, far more of the road across Organsdale Field was once visible. But what disuse began, the plough has since completed. The raised agger *that carried the metalled surface has long since disappeared; though the* fossae, *or ditches, were still detectable in Victorian times. Occasional patches of compacted, potato-sized pebbles jutting through the surface may be parts of the original Roman surface.*

While the path curves right to follows the field edge, the line of the Roman road ran straight on, slightly downslope.

Almost ½ mile/1 kilometre from the clump of Scots pines and oaks, the path crosses a stile. Ignore the narrow gate that enters

Gypsy caravans were once a common sight in Delamere Forest

the new plantations on Hangingstone Hill immediately on the right. Instead, go straight on, towards the edge of the old forest close to Kings Chair—still almost on the line of the old Roman road.

The field on your the left is called Organsdale. Look carefully and the route of the Roman road becomes clear once more as a broad platform cut into the hill. As the road leaves Organsdale field, there are the vestiges of a bank on either side. Towards the forest edge, a sandstone outcrop has been cut back to allow the road to pass; and the road follows the contour of the slope into the trees. Imagine the thousands of people who have passed this way over the centuries: Celtic warriors, Roman legionaries, carters taking stone to build medieval Vale Royal Abbey, drovers, soldiers, labourers, lords, foot travellers and horsemen.

5. At the bottom of Organsdale field, climb over the stile into the forest. Within 50 metres, the path joins a broad forest track rising from the main A54. Turn right, uphill, away from the road.

Opposite the junction of paths here, the line of the Roman road can still be traced as it runs on down towards Kelsall. When this section was excavated, a 10 feet/3 metres deep, and 36 feet/12 metres wide channel was found cut into the rock. Today, traces of the banks on either side can be seen among the trees.

Here too, is the site of a fork in the Roman road, the parting of the ways for Manchester and Middlewich. It's a place once known as Hinds Well. *The Middlewich (Salinis) road lines up with a toll cottage on the A54, and merges with the modern road to Winsford (at the modern junction!) about ½mile/1 kilometre away.*

Continue gently uphill on the broad, sandy forestry track; it's part of the Sandstone Trail.

Two hundred metres on, at the top of the slope on the right are the shallow medieval quarries of Kings Chair, reputed to have been the source of stone for Vale Royal Abbey, erected between 1277-1300.

As the path curves uphill, look for the steel and terracotta Sandstone Trail waymarker in the shape of a wild boar. This is Nettleford Wood; the 'ford' part of the name comes from the Celtic Welsh for way or road, *fford*—a telltale clue to the nearby presence of the Roman road.

At the top of the rise, turn right on a permissive path signposted to 'Pale Heights'. A second signpost states: 'Sandstone Trail—Alternative Route'. The surfaced path swings to the right and then left, before passing through a gap in the old hedge. It then rises to run along the flat top of the hill, with three BT and Civil Defence microwave masts dominating the hilltop above.

This is the Old Pale, an area first enclosed from Delamere Forest in 1338 on the orders of Edward Ill, 'to make a chamber in the forest for the preservation of vert and venison.' *The pale itself was a tall encircling fence erected to enclose and protect the deer. The head forester's house, known in old documents as the* Chamber in the Forest, *once stood close to Iron Age Eddisbury hillfort.*

When the path forks, beyond another gap in a hedge, turn right, uphill towards the masts.

Once at the top, go straight ahead on a concrete service road, keeping the fence and masts to your left.

From the breezy summit, the panoramic views take in the Welsh hills, the Dee estuary, the Wirral peninsula, Stanlow oil refinery, the Mersey estuary, Liverpool Anglican Cathedral, Fiddlers Ferry power station, the Pennines and the Peak District. Only the view to the south is disappointing.

Beyond the crest, head downhill from the masts on a tarmaced track. Directly ahead in the middle distance is Eddisbury Hillfort. Seen from this side, the flattened ovoid shape and full extent of the fort becomes clear. High on its sandstone plateau, it dominates the ridge and the country beyond. No wonder it was a strategic stronghold for so long.

Less than 200 metres downhill from the masts, turn left, off the tarmaced road and onto a narrower surfaced path that skirts the top of the hill. Now the masts rise up to the left.

At the next T-junction of paths, 200 metres on, go left again, back onto the hilltop ridge.

At the next junction, go right. The path regains the top of the Old Pale before winding downhill again, back towards the edge of the old forest.

Among the forest trees below, notice the large recently flooded Blakemere lake. Clear felling of a substantial area in the 1990s allowed water to refill the old mossland.

Continue downhill on the grit-surfaced path through gaps in two old hedgelines to rejoin the broad track at the base of the hill. At the bottom, turn left, to meet the broad, limestone surfaced forestry track that we crossed on the outward journey.

Turn left along the track towards Eddisbury Lodge. Forty-five metres or so beyond the lodge, turn right on to the Sandstone Trail, signposted for Barnesbridge Gate. Enter the forest, recross the Manchester-Chester railway line, and retrace the outward route to complete the walk.

7. Peckforton

From the Stone Elephant to The Pheasant

Cheshire's own 'Elephant and Castle', cobbled estate track, ancient saltway over the hills, haunted bridge, panoramic views and a Gospel Oak

Start: *Peckforton, 4 miles/6.5 kilometres south-west of Tarporley. Map reference: SJ 538566.*

Distance: *2¹/₂ miles/4 kilometres.*

Duration: *Allow 1¹/₂ –2 hours.*

Difficulty: *Steady climb to ridge. Cobbled estate track, sandy lane and rough pasture. Usually dry.*

Food and Drink: *The Pheasant Inn, Higher Burwardsley. Free House. Real ales. Hot and cold food every day. Accommodation available. 01829 770434.*

Maps: *OS 1:25,000 Explorer 257 Crewe and Nantwich; OS 1:50,000 Landranger 117 Chester, Wrexham and surrounding area.*

AT PECKFORTON, beneath the shadow of Cheshire's wooded central sandstone ridge, two rivers begin within a stone's throw of each other. While the Weaver snakes south before looping north just inside the Cheshire-Shropshire border near Audlem, the tiny, less well known Gowy meanders north for 19 miles/30 kilometres, past Beeston Castle, and across the Cheshire farmlands, to flow into the Mersey near Stanlow refinery.

The cradle of both rivers is the small area between Peckforton Mere and Peckforton Moss—once a swampy wasteland, but now open farmland, much of it reclaimed since the 1840s. Between the Mere, the Moss and the hills lies the picturesque village of Peckforton with its tiny black and white cottages, some of which date from the 16th century. For fascinating information and images of the village and the surrounding hills, see the excellent www.peckfortonhills.co.uk.

The walk

The walk begins just over a mile / 1.5 kilometres from the A49, on Stone House Lane, close to the centre of Peckforton village. Park on the wide verge opposite the end of Hill Lane. Alternatively, turn right a little farther on, into Quarrybank, where a sign points to 'Peckforton and Beeston Village Hall'. Past the old estate sawmill, now a private house, is a large, tree-shaded car park for the village hall and 'Exhibition Centre', from which wooden steps lead downhill onto Hill Lane.

This is a lovely walk for summer evenings: across the hills to the Pheasant Inn. Enjoy a quiet pint or two; watch the sun set over the Welsh hills; return in the gloaming with bats and owls nimble overhead.

Until the mid 1800s the village had almost twice the number of houses it does today; in 1841 there were 61, compared to the current 34. Many of the scattered black and white cottages are thatched; look for the reed finials on two roofs—they're crafted in the shape of pheasants.

Close to the village centre, and next to the old sawmill, is Laundry Cottage. Behind its neat holly hedge, silhouetted among the bright flowers, is one of Cheshire's most unusual oddities: a 12 foot/4 metres high, carved sandstone elephant with a castle on its back.

1. From the elephant, follow the road for 50 metres towards Beeston Castle, or descend the steps from the car park, and turn left up narrow Hill Lane.

The tiny black and white house opposite Hill Lane was the old blacksmith's shop; today it's still called Smithy Cottage. A sign at the gate offers 'Free Range Eggs'. Close behind the smithy was Peckforton Mill, a water mill whose wheel was powered by the infant River Gowy.

Evidence of a far older people using the area was turned up in 1901, when a local farmer found a Neolithic stone-hammer in a cart load of clover from a nearby field. Finely polished, and 4½ inches/11 centimetres long, it had been made of Cumberland granite and traded here, on ancient trackways along the hills, around 5,000-6,000 years ago.

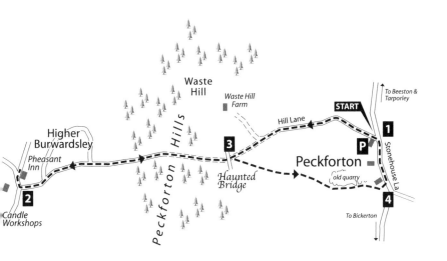

Hill Lane winds uphill between steep banks clad in ferns and cow parsley.

Overhanging damson trees in autumn fill the road with purple windfallen fruit. A silence, broken only by the crowing of a distant cockerel, evokes a rural past when every lane in this part of Cheshire was just as narrow. Local reminiscences tell of the horses of the hunt leaping clear over the lanes from bank to bank.

Until the 1830s there were at least four cottages on Hill Lane; only one is left, now renamed 'Treetops'—a house that until its 'restoration' and re-roofing in the 1990s had spiky houseleeks covering part of its roof. For centuries, houseleeks were deliberately placed on roofs in the firm belief that they could prevent lightning strikes.

A little further on, beyond the recently created gardens with their laid hawthorn hedges on the left, is a small, hedged-in hollow on the right, the site of one of the vanished homes. Only frail dog rose, docks and white-umbelled cow parsleys mark the spot today.

Soon the track begins to climb more steeply. Although now carpeted with tarmac, until the late 1990s the lane was surfaced with crude sandstone blocks interspersed with old tree trunks laid across the track to slow the winter streams.

The Peckforton Stone Elephant

ONE OF CHESHIRE'S ODDEST CURIOSITIES, the 'Elephant and Castle' at Peckforton was carved in 1859 by John Watson, a stonemason working on Victorian Peckforton Castle. The sandstone for both came from the same local quarry. Over 12 feet/4 metres high, the elephant with its odd fringed ears, is carved from a single block of stone, the castle on its back from three separate pieces.

When it was new, the hollow, turreted castle had glass in every one of its windows. The impressive carving was intended to be used as a beehive; though there is no evidence that it ever was.

An elephant with a castle on its back featured in the coat of arms of the Corbett family, who were owners of Peckforton until about 1626.

Between the wars an attempt was made to buy the carving and ship it to America; happily the owners resisted the lure of Yankee dollars, and the elephant remained in its native Cheshire.

In summer, sunlight filtering through the aerial leaves of tall oaks, beeches and sycamores dapples the ground. Tawny owls shelter in the trees above; come this way at dusk and you may hear them scuffling about in the branches overhead, or see a dark silhouette wafting out over the fields to hunt. Even during the day the path is sometimes crossed by the rank, sharp must of a hunting fox—a distinctive country smell.

Towards the top, two narrower tracks branch off to the right; they lead to secluded Waste Hill Farm, once known as the Pheasantry, where the head gamekeeper for the Peckforton Estates lived. The adjoining kennels have since vanished. Today, metal signs nailed to the trees just off the track proclaim: 'Peckforton Estate. Strictly Private. No Right of Way'.

Beyond the junction, the lane's surface deteriorates. It's as if it's slipping back in time. To make the climb easier for horse-drawn carts, the track was surfaced with locally quarried sandstone. Look for the gutters down either side; and then see how, despite this, a century of rains has eroded meandering gullies between the stones.

At the top a solidly built stone bridge crosses Hill Lane.

Listen for the echo underneath. Known locally as the Haunted Bridge, the story goes that a ghostly servant woman walks from the ruins of a stone hut—still visible among the trees on the right past the bridge—along the sandy track and up the bank on the far side; under her arm she carries her own severed head. Local superstition says that if you see her you'll be dead within the year.

An early photograph of the Peckforton elephant with its tusks still intact, not long after it was carved in 1859

The bridge was built in the 1850s to take horse-drawn carriages from the newly built Peckforton Castle to the gatehouse at the Peckforton Gap. Before that, it carried a light railway-line used to ferry building-stone to the Castle from the specially created Firbank Quarry, deep in the woods on the left.

Beyond the bridge the track becomes sandy and levels out.

Outcrops of the underlying sandstone, worn smooth by generations of cartwheels and feet, push up through the path. The area to the right is called Waste Hill and reflects the time when these hills were viewed as useless for agriculture.

This sunny, open part of the track follows an ancient route over the Peckforton Hills. Leading directly from Alpraham, Bunbury, and Spurstow to Burwardsley, Tattenhall and then Chester, it was part of the 'Walesmansway' *or* 'Walchmonstreet'—*Welshman's way,* 'a route for the trade in salt between the Cheshire 'wiches' [*salt towns*] and Wales.' *Local Peckforton people, too, regularly walked this way to Chester market—a round trip of roughly 28 miles/45 kilometres.*

At dusk on a warm summer's evenings the lane is filled with tiny bats, pipistrelles—Cheshire 'Bit bats'—patrolling their figure-of-eight beats for insects. Listen carefully and you may hear their high-pitched echo-location calls.

Soon the sandy track tilts imperceptibly downhill, past an estate-worker's house. Go through the gateway that straddles the track, leaving the Borough of Crewe and Nantwich behind. The lane is once more metalled, and slopes more steeply.

Continue downhill past two hugely enlarged old farmworkers cottages: white-painted 'Elephant Track, Burwardsley' cottage, and prim 'Rock Cottage'. The lane, icy here in winter, cuts through the bedrock, 12 feet/3.5 metres deep in places, and winds on downhill past attractive hilltop Rock House Farm.

At the next junction the wide panorama of the Cheshire Plain opens out ahead—a patchwork of green fields edged by trees—towards Wales and the River Dee.

2. Continue, until another, muddled, junction of lanes by a house.

Go right, downhill on Fowlers Bench Lane, for 50 metres, and then right again.

Ahead is the lovely, no longer out-of-the-way Pheasant Inn at Higher Burwardsley, a former black and white farmhouse with a block for mounting horses still outside.

Not so long ago it was still known as the Carden Arms, after the old Cheshire Carden family. The pub and its terraces and beer garden are a good place from which to watch the sun set behind the distant Welsh mountains; and if it's raining, it's a relaxing spot to while away an hour or two.

Nearby is the popular Candle Factory with its demonstrations, shop and tearoom.

From the Pheasant Inn, refreshed, retrace you steps until you come to the Haunted Bridge. At most times of the year there is enough light to see by even when the sun has gone down; and it makes for a pleasant evening stroll. But don't linger by the bridge too long.

3. Immediately past the bridge, on the right, a double stile climbs into the adjacent fields; it's signposted 'Stonehouse Lane, Bulkeley'. The view opens out to the east, with the Peak District hills blue on the horizon.

An ancient lane called 'Baws Lane' originally ran from here, along the forest edge and on down to Stonehouse Farm, on the Bulkeley road. Several cottages edged the lane; and it was in the garden of one of these cottages that the stone elephant once stood. It was moved to its present position in about 1890, when the cottages were demolished.

But for us, another footpath runs on ahead, diagonally downhill across the pasture. Head for the two oaks just visible in mid-field, peeping over the brow of the hill.

Little owls, introduced into Cheshire in the 1890s, can sometimes be seen perched in their branches. The hill is popular, too, as a sledge run in winter, when the steep bluff at the bottom can prove treacherous.

Follow the slope down towards the large clump of trees at the bottom.

Through a field gateway, look down to the left into the now disused quarry where sandstone was cut for the local houses; it's at least 40 feet/12.5 metres deep with sheer sides, and full of shadow, scrub and brambles.

We are once more on 'Walesmansway', a route used by, among others, the famous itinerant preacher, John Wesley. He preached at Bunbury and the surrounding villages—said to be the birthplace of Primitive Methodism in Cheshire—in October 1749.

Beyond another stile, look for a massive oak tree on the left. A gnarled leviathan with a giant trunk, it is at least 16 feet/5 metres in circumference. John Wesley is said to have preached beneath its, even then, ancient branches. When this was part of the old way over the hills, leading up via Peckforton Hall Lane from the ancient salt town of Nantwich and on into Wales, the route passed a number of churches and chapels on its way.

Two further stiles, one a curious oak and sandstone ladder, take us through a dense plantation to Bank Cottages, with their ancient pear trees, chrysanthemums and neat potato patches, back into Peckforton village.

4. Once back out on the road, turn left; your car is less than 100 metres ahead.

Look for the Victorian post box built into the wall, with its telltale ornate VR on the front. It's another reminder of the history of Peckforton. But before you leave, think how pleasant it would be if the black and white cottage on the corner was still used for its original purpose: it used to be another pub—called the White Horse. And all its beer was home brewed.

8. Bickerton

From Mad Allen's Hole to Maiden Castle

Hermit's cave, memorial stone, Iron Age hillfort, views, breezes and bilberries

Start: *Bickerton, 4 miles/6 kilometres north of Malpas. Map reference: SJ 510536.*

Distance: *2¹/₂ miles/4 kilometres.*

Duration: *Allow 2 hours.*

Difficulty: *Long but gentle ascent to ridge, undulating hilltop, dry sandy paths; usually dry.*

Food and Drink: *Bickerton Poacher, Wrexham Road, Bickerton. Freehouse. Good food, bar snacks, restaurant. Disabled access and toilet facilities. Children welcome. 01829 720226.*

Maps: *OS 1:25,000 Explorer 257 Crewe and Nantwich; OS 1:50,000 Landranger 117 Chester, Wrexham and surrounding area.*

BEES HUM OVER THE HEATHER on these high hills, an echo of a distant time when the local names Bickley and Bickerton meant 'Bee-keeper's Field' and 'Bee-keeper's Farm'. Generations later, in Norman times, the name was still *Bicretone*—a bee-sounding word. On a summer's afternoon, the drone of insects replaces the drum of cars and seems to carry the hills back in time. For a moment the clock is arrested and it could be any afternoon in history.

The Bickerton Hills are formed of overlying, tilted beds of sandstone: Keuper and Bunter Mottled Sandstones, Pebble Beds and Waterstones. Created at the bottom of a shallow sea some 225 million years ago, during the Triassic period, and then tilted upwards, the rocks were later scoured by glaciers during successive Ice Ages. The softer rocks became valleys; the harder rocks became hills.

When early man arrived, the Cheshire valleys were still covered with peat mosses and marshland, formed by water collecting in the undrained glacial boulder clays. In contrast, the sandstone hills seemed a hospitable place: high and dry, with easily tilled soils, open mixed oak-woodland and springs of clear water, bubbling up from the aptly named Waterstones at their foot. Six of the early Iron Age hillforts recognised in Cheshire occupy high points along the ridge; in those days the hills were the place to be.

The walk

The walk starts at the tiny village of Bickerton, stretched along the dip slope of the hills, 4 miles/6.5 kilometres north of Malpas. Turn off the A534 Wrexham to Nantwich road as it crests the gap between the Bickerton and Bulkeley hills, not far from Gallantry Bank. Still known locally as Salters Lane, the A534 was one of the old salt roads running from Nantwich into Wales. Now, an old cast-iron sign points to 'Bickerton Church', 'Cholmondeley 4' and 'Malpas 4½'.

At the bottom of the hill, cross the Broxton to Cholmondeley road into Goldford Lane, and park on a triangle of gravel just past Bickerton church.

Until 1843, Bickerton was part of the huge parish of Malpas, with its 25 townships. Holy Trinity church, built in 1839, is a 'chapel of ease'—so called because it meant the villagers no longer had to travel long distances to church on a Sunday. The one acre cemetery was added later on, in 1880. Today the straggling village of Bickerton is still attractive; and three signs on a post by the churchyard wall boast: 'Best Kept Village 1977, 1981, 1982'.

1. Opposite the church, a sign points uphill to 'Larkton Hill and Whitchurch' on the Sandstone Trail, beside beech-hedged 'Bickerton Croft' house. Nearby, a blue metal case displays a map and information about the Trail.

For the next mile/1.5 kilometres, we follow the Sandstone Trail with its symbol of a black footprint on a yellow ground. Go through a wooden kissing gate to enter the National Trust's 'Bickerton Hill'.

Ahead, the sandy path winds uphill through mixed oak and birch woodland. Orange-berried rowans startle the eye; while outcrops of sandstone and gnarled roots, worn smooth by walkers, push up through the thin soil.

A hundred metres on, the path snakes around a deep pit to the right.

It's a small local quarry where hand-cut sandstone blocks were dug for houses and farm buildings. The large shed in the field nearby to the right is a helicopter hangar; look for the concrete apron in front, and the wind sock—to tell the pilot the pre-take-off wind direction— on the brow of the hill beyond.

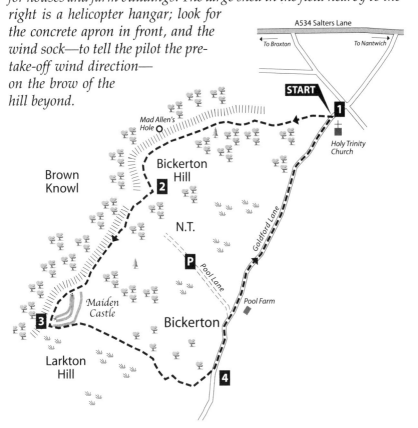

A hundred metres later, go through a second wooden kissing gate. Follow the waymarked path as it meanders gently uphill beneath the birches.

When the path starts to climb more steeply, the feet of innumerable walkers have worn a deep defile into the slope, showing how the old hollow ways were created. Carefully 'pitched' stone steps have been put in by the National Trust to combat this erosion.

At the top, go straight ahead. Soon the path levels, climbs, then levels out again. And then, on the right as we approach the summit, hints of the impressive view beyond appear between the trunks—a flickering panorama like some Victorian *zoetrope* or picture-making toy.

The path dips alongside an overhanging sandstone cliff. It's a good place to shelter in a downpour. Over the years unthinking yoofs *have carved their names and initials into the soft sandstone: 'Alex', 'PIG', 'Dave + Sal 72' and naughty 'Deborah'.*

Down the slippery briar and fern clad slope to the right here is Mad Allen's Hole, a curious man-made cave cut into the cliff. To reach it requires a wild scramble through the brambles, and is only for the hardy. Halfway down the slope, go around the cliff face to the right. The large, two level cave is hidden behind a huge moss-grown slab that has crashed down from the rock-face above, and is difficult to find.

Mad Allen's Hole is said to have been occupied by a young man who lost his sanity when both sets of parents objected to his marriage to the girl he loved. He shunned society, sold all his belongings, and retired to a cave where he died seventy years later.

In fact, he moved several times, from one cave to another, as a letter in an old Cheshire newspaper suggests:

'In or about the year 1809 ... strange stories were afoot as to a hermit who had been discovered in Allenscombe's Cave, in the parish of Harthill; that he had secreted himself there, as he had previously done in a similar cave near to Carden cliff. After remaining a self-made alien in his own country for so long, the whereabouts of his hermitage was accidentally discovered, and the sanctity of his rocky home was soon invaded by strangers.'

Local children often skipped school in early July to pick bilberries on the open heathland on the Peckforton, Bulkeley and Bickerton Hills

It would seem that, irritated by these invasions, he moved to the Bickerton cave—Mad Allen's Hole—only towards the end of his life.

Another source offers a more prosaic interpretation. It claims, '... the name is taken from a man hired by a local landlord to impersonate a hermit in an artificial cave here.' *It's not such a far-fetched claim; an 18th century fad for the picturesque meant rich patrons* did *sometimes fill their estates with hermits and grottoes. You must choose your favourite story.*

On along the edge, the path opens onto heathland dotted with rowans and small oaks.

Purple and mauve heather and ling contrast with the emerald bracken and almost luminous green young bilberries; and swallows and martins swirl above the lip of the scarp in summer. Except on the calmest of days, the breeze that beats in over the edge from the Welsh hills dominates the senses.

And the view ...! It's a delight. To the north the line of the hills stretches past Raw Head and Harthill to Kelsall, Delamere, Frodsham and Helsby. On the distant Mersey, look for the Fiddlers Ferry power-

station cooling towers and further round, on the horizon, the vast tower of Liverpool's Anglican Cathedral. Around to the left, the panorama takes in Chester and the Welsh hills—including Jubilee Tower-topped Moel Famau—and, in front, the broad farmlands of the valley of the Dee. Use the OS map to work out other landmarks.

Close to the highest point, a memorial stone, known locally as Kitty's Stone, displays poems in tribute to a lost partner and long-gone summer days.

Below, close to the bottom of the hill, are a line of springs and wells that have supplied water since time immemorial. More recently, between 1946 and 1954, deep boreholes were sunk by the Staffordshire Potteries Water Board to supply water to the Birmingham conurbation; small square brick buildings covering the boreholes can be seen along the spring line between Bickerton and the Peckforton Pumping Station. As a result, many far older local wells and springs are now dry; and the water table has sunk alarmingly.

Aerial surveys made during the drought summer of 1976 showed an undefended Bronze Age settlement close to Rawhead, just to the north; and a possible Roman signalling station nearby. Both are further evidence of the attraction of this area to early man.

The path curves along the top of the hill, and then downhill out of the wind.

Here, the delicate woody scent of the heather evokes the summer moorlands and mountains of a lifetime.

2. A hundred and fifty metres or so later, a tall Sandstone Trail signpost points right, down a broad, well used sandy track to 'Larkton Hill'. Shortly, it meets another, still broader track running up from Bickerton, and on over the hill, signposted to 'Brown Knoll'. We go straight over, uphill again, following the sign for 'Larkton Hill and Whitchurch'.

When the path forks, bear right, up a sharp slope made easier by crude stone steps. Over the crest is an undulating, still rising plateau.

In the early 1900s, the hills were cropped by sheep. But by the 1980s and '90s, the area was dense with birch scrub and bracken. Now National Trust volunteers are sensitively clearing the trees to help

Kitty's Stone, above Brown Knowl, is a sandstone memorial to a lost partner

restore this rare lowland heath. *Adders, lizards and bilberries are returning once more. If the snakes are elusive, these hills are nonetheless one of the best places in Cheshire for the tiny subtle-flavoured fruits. The low, dark green bushes are covered with purple-blue berries (in reality, they're not berries but the expanded calyx of the flower) in early July. Some years are better than others. In the best years even the birds glut themselves; and their lurid purple droppings decorate the sandstone outcrops and paths with abstract splashes.*

The path climbs steadily along the edge, then dips down to skirt a small indentation in the slope.

At the top of the next rise, 694 feet/216 metres above sea-level, is the Iron Age hillfort of Maiden Castle. Heather and birch scrub hide the earthworks today, and many walkers are unaware of the existence of the fort 'whose turfed and cowslipped ramparts seems, more hill than history, ageless and oblivion blurred.'

Unfortunately, the continuing success of the Sandstone Trail has slowly eroded the ramparts; as late as 1819, the Cheshire historian Ormerod noted the '... perfect state of the works.' Only in 1982 was the land given to The National Trust; urgent remedial work was done to protect the hillfort's fragile archaeology, and now the hillfort should be safe.

Where the steep edge—quarried for building stone long after the Iron Age—peters out, we cross the defences again, and drop down crude sandstone steps to open heather and bilberry heathland dotted with occasional birch.

Embedded in a boulder beside the ramparts here, a National Trust plaque recaps the hillfort's history.

3. The path splits off in three directions; we go left, away from the edge.

This area was re-cleared only a few years ago, to form a semi-open area of lowland heath: an increasingly scarce habitat in Britain. Already this has attracted the rare nightjar or 'goatsucker'—a nocturnal, moth-eating, migrant bird—back to these summer hills.

Archaeological excavation of Maiden Castle's northern ramparts in 1934-5 uncovered the remains of massive earthworks faced with drystone walling, featuring an inturned entrance with guard chamber

Maiden Castle: An Iron Age Hillfort

MAIDEN CASTLE IS AN ANCIENT HILLFORT rather than a castle; and was a defended village of the Iron Age *Cornovii* tribe in the centuries before the Roman conquest.

Precipices defend the diminutive 1.5 acre/0.6 hectare hillfort to the northwest; whilst two curving ramparts, each with its own ditch, protect the shallow south-eastern slopes. Excavations by Liverpool University, in 1934-35 and again in 1962, showed the inner bank was originally 17 feet/5 metres wide and 12 feet/4 metres high, with some kind of palisade along the top. Massive drystone walling supported a bank of sand and boulders interlaced with deliberately charred branches. The outer rampart had a similar drystone wall at the front but not at the back.

The main entrance was an inturned sunken passage with a cobbled surface, which pierced both banks on the north-east side. It was defended by at least one pair of stout gates and a guard chamber.

Quarrying for stone inside the fort, sometime in recent history, has obliterated much of the original ground surface; but traces survive of large circular houses built probably of wattle and daub, with thatched roofs and south-east facing porches designed to catch the warmth of the early morning sun.

The people who lived in them were farmers and hunters, who perhaps traded in salt and pottery. Much like the Gaulish tribes in Julius Caesar's accounts, the men probably indulged in seasonal ritualised warfare, while the women did most of the work.

Maiden Castle is an old name, *Maegden* Castle, meaning a virgin or untaken stronghold. However, local folklore makes the charming suggestion that, in the absence of their men, the fort was once defended by women alone.

Fifty metres on, the hillfort's still imposing double ramparts curve away into the bracken and heather to the left, splashed with the vibrant yellow of gorse in flower.

No horses are allowed on the fort, but hoof prints pattern the adjacent broad sandy track as it snakes downhill along the edge of the birch woods.

Once under the trees, the track passes rough pasture to the right. At the bottom of the slope, go through a wooden kissing gate. Soon afterwards, the track bends right, around the bottom of the field; fifty metres later it meets a dogleg in a gravelled lane.

Go left, downhill. The lane sweeps left, then right, then left again, around the honeysuckle-entwined hedges of three large houses with small names like 'The Cottage'. And suddenly a new view appears: ahead are the Peak District hills, while looming on the southern horizon is the vast bulk of the Wrekin, away in Shropshire.

4. At the bottom of the slope, the gravelled track comes out on Goldford Lane. Turn left past a loose group of tiny cottages lost in lush flower gardens.

Two hundred metres on, the narrow lane reaches an open area opposite Pool Farm, where tall hornbeams overhang a silted up farm pond on which white water lilies grew within living memory. From here a sandy track, called Pool Lane, signposted to 'Bickerton Hill, Sandstone Trail', makes an attractive alternative route to Maiden Castle.

But we continue along Goldford Lane, past Hill Farm and Hill Top. And on past the old fashioned wooden scout hut of the 1st Bickerton Scout Group. Above them all, to the left, rise the green birch woods of the Bickerton Hills.

Half-a-mile/1 kilometre later, and we are back at Bickerton church and the end of our walk. It's a charming part of Cheshire. So let's go round again, to Mad Allen's Hole, the hillfort, the bilberries and the view. It won't take long.

9. Tushingham
A Dead Duck and Diploma

Ancient half-timbered inn, ghostly duck, Cavalier's hat, isolated chapel and horse drawn hearse, lost Roman and medieval roads, rare Roman bronze diploma, and a bottomless pit

Start: *Bell o' th' Hill, 3 miles/5 kilometres north of Whitchurch. Map reference: SJ 523454.*

Distance: *4 miles/6.5 kilometres.*

Duration: *Allow 2 hours.*

Difficulty: *Flat or gently undulating. Lanes and footpaths across pasture. Sandy and mostly dry; some muddy sections.*

Food and Drink: *The Blue Bell, Bell o' th' Hill, Tushingham. Free House. Hand pulled beers; guest ales. Bar snacks and full meals, lunchtimes and evenings. Children welcome. 01948 662172.*

Maps: *OS 1:25,000 Explorer 257 Crewe and Nantwich; OS 1:50,000 Landranger 117 Chester, Wrexham and surrounding area.*

'Cheshire's Deep South' is the apt title of one of the County's old tourist brochures describing the area south of a line from Wrexham to Crewe. The clever phrase conjures up an image of hicks and hillbillies, corn bread and catfish from the American south. But the Cheshire that abuts the North Wales Borderlands and Shropshire is famous for other things: for its pastoral beauty, its black and white houses, its canals and cheese. One of the finest dairy farming areas in Britain, south Cheshire has more cows to the acre than anywhere else in the world; or at least it did in the days before EU milk quotas and the oppressive hand of the supermarkets squeezed our dairy farmers dry.

Friesian cows, the familiar and ubiquitous high-yielding black and white dairy cattle, are still common in the oak-punctuated pastures. Though most of the famous Cheshire cheese is today made in creameries, some local farms still produce the top quality 'Farmhouse' cheese

Greener, quieter, and more fertile than north Cheshire, the south has an equally long, though perhaps less well documented, history. It seems steeped in the past; and even the Romans were here—as we shall discover.

The walk

The walk begins 18 miles/29 kilometres south of Chester, and 3 miles/5 kilometres north of Whitchurch, just inside the Cheshire border, at a tiny village called Bell o' th' Hill. Turn off the Chester to Whitchurch road—the A 41, just past the tall Victorian church at Tushingham. A new stretch of fast road bypasses the old village; and the narrow loops of the old A41 seem unnaturally quiet. It's as if the new road has by-passed time, too, and carried a small island of Cheshire back into its rural past.

Park close to the 'Blue Bell Inn', a large half-timbered building on a bend in the road.

It is one of the oldest inns in Cheshire. Ogilby's Britannia Roadbook, *published in 1675, when this was the main highway from Chester to Whitchurch, Shrewsbury, Ludlow and Bristol, calls it* 'Ye signe of Ye Bel'. *There are few houses here even today; and until the 1950s, according to the Women's Institute of the time, this tiny hamlet had,* 'no mains water, no sewerage, no electricity, no telephone kiosk, no Post Office, no surgery and no new houses'.

Inside, the ancient 'Blue Bell Inn' is as yet unspoilt. Low doorways connect a maze of rooms, and the main bar features an inglenook fireplace. On the walls are old photographs and a miscellany of outmoded farm implements: rick cutters, pail yokes and dung forks; while in a case are a leather Cavalier's hat, and a 400 years old mummified rat that was found curled in a wall cavity.

Stranger still is the tale of the resident ghost, not of a human but of a duck! A fluffy duckling was brought up in a basket by the fire, but as

One of the oldest pubs in Cheshire, the half-timbered 'Blue Bell Inn' at Bell o' th' Hill is shown in Ogilby's 1675 Britannia Roadbook

it grew so it became more territorial. It pecked at people's ankles until eventually it was killed and buried at the bottom of the cellar stairs. But neither the step nor the duck would 'stay put'. And having escaped, the ghostly duck would run about making a nuisance of itself in the old way, pecking spectrally at people's ankles. So twelve parsons were called in to 'pray it down'. Each held a lighted candle, and as they prayed the duck got smaller and smaller, until it could be popped into a bottle. The bottle was tightly corked and bricked up in a wall. And, by all accounts, it's still there today, with the duck's ghost inside. Whisky is not the only spirit in this pub.

1. Leaving the 'Blue Bell Inn', with the building behind you, turn right and follow the curves of the now mud-bespattered and almost deserted old A41. Three hundred metres later, turn right up a narrow, sunken lane signposted 'Sandstone Trail'. Much of the route follows the Sandstone Trail with its distinctive waymarkers that show a black boot print in a yellow circle.

Isolated Old St Chad's chapel occupies an ancient, perhaps pre-Saxon site

Within 50 metres the lane meets the new by-pass; cross carefully, it's a fast and busy road.

Beyond the new A41, the surfaced lane continues out into the fields, and the roar of traffic soon fades away.

Eight species of native tree or bush can be found in the hedges on either side here; and, in places, even though the ground is level, the lane is 2 feet/60 centimetres below field level. Celandines and wild arum dot the hedgerows in spring. Bluebells and dogs mercury grow beneath the hedge—both are so-called 'ancient woodland indicators'. All of which suggest the lane's antiquity.

At the lane's abrupt end, 500 metres later, go through the wooden kissing gate. The lane didn't always end here; when the old Tithe Map was surveyed in 1838 the lane continued via Barhill Farm to Gorstyhill Cottages—the latter stretch of which, as we shall see, is still a bridleway today.

Beyond the gate, a broad grassy track reaches out across the open field.

The tumbled remains of Denhall Quay, Neston (Walk 1)

Parkgate promenade from the Dee Estuary (Walk 1)

St Peter's Church framed by willows, Plemstall (Walk 2)

An unusual family box tomb at Plemstall (Walk 2)

Hockenhull Platts packhorse bridges near Tarvin (Walk 3)

Dawn mists overlooking Delamere Forest (Walk 6)

Looking across Little Budworth Mere (Walk 10)

Through the sunlit forest, Delamere (Walk 6)

On the ridgeway below the Old Pale, Eddisbury (Walk 6)

A medieval half-timbered house at Peckforton (Walk 7)

A swathe of fragrant Cheshire bluebells

Urchin's Kitchen, a glacial meltwater gorge in Primrosehill Wood (Walk 5)

Isolated St Edith's Church at Shocklach (Walk 4)

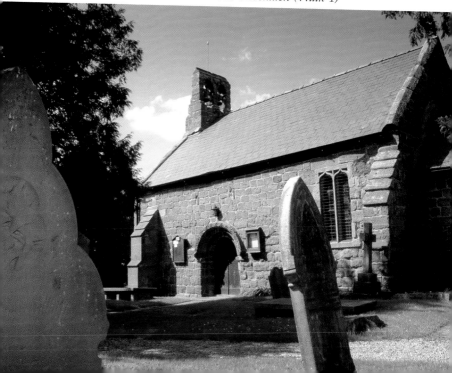

Disused truck incline at Kerridge End, Bollington (Walk 14)

White Nancy, the famous folly above Bollington (Walk 14)

Old Saint Chad's, Tushingham

TUSHINGHAM WAS PART OF THE ANCIENT PARISH OF MALPAS, one of the largest medieval parishes in the County. Because it was so large, chapels of ease like St. Chad's were built to save people an over-long Sunday walk.

During the nineteenth century the medieval parishes were subdivided. A new Victorian church, again dedicated to St. Chad, was built on the main road between 1860-63, leaving the old chapel stranded in the fields. The new church has no graveyard, and old St. Chad's remains the parish burial ground. The shape and character of the burial ground suggest it may be of Saxon origin.

A far older timber-framed church originally stood on the site; it may have been a chantry chapel, as fields nearby are still called the Chantry Fields. In 1689 it was rebuilt in brick using money given by a local man who had made good in London.

With no heating or lighting, monthly services are held here only during the summer. The most popular is Rushbearing Day in August—an ancient ceremony, when freshly cut rushes are strewn on the floor.

Old St. Chad's inaccessibility is unusual. But Ogilby's 1675 route map shows that the old road from Whitchurch to Chester once ran further to the east than the 18th century turnpike (or toll road) that replaced it, and which is now the modern A41. The old road has long since been ploughed.

Look carefully at the topography of the land and you'll notice how the chapel sits on a tongue of dry land above the old, boggy lowlands. The sloping field behind the chapel is called Hollywell Ridding, and there's an ancient pond at the bottom; perhaps the name hints at early Celtic water worship at a holy well or spring. This may have been a sacred site long before the Romans came.

Rolling countryside, latticed with hedges and punctuated by tall ashes and oaks, spreads away to the south and east. In summer, swallows flit in low arcs across the grass, hawking for flies. This undulating pasture is real brown hare country; with their jacked-up back legs and black-tipped ears, these native animals are easily distinguished from the rabbits that are also abundant here.

As the ice sheet retreated northwards at the end of the last Ice Age, a vast meltwater lake covered the lower ground away to the south-east and east. Today, remnants of this ancient lake remain as picturesque Barmere, Marbury Mere and Quiosley Mere; and for thousands of years, the area below was a vast and intractable bog.

Nestled among cherry, yew and cedar trees on the far side of the field, is lonely Chad's chapel. Enter the carefully rabbit-proofed churchyard through the white-painted wicket gate. The garage-like building on the left was originally a meeting house; it now protects the old horse-drawn parish hearse—once known locally as the 'Black Maria'. Church owls—now better known as barn owls—nested in the secluded belfry within living memory; sadly they no longer do. But perhaps the old superstition, that to see one close to the village is an omen of an impending death, is still held locally? Today, a pair of noisy ravens nest in one of the lofty cedars behind the chapel.

2. Leaving the ancient churchyard, strike out diagonally, across the field. Head for the stile and signpost visible halfway along the distant hedge. Once at the stile, a Sandstone Trail signpost points back towards the chapel. The Marches Way continues straight ahead, towards the tower of St Chad's church at Tushingham; but we bear right, heading north, along the hedge line, on the Sandstone Trail.

Four stiles later, the path emerges on a farm lane by the tall, white farmhouse at Barhill Developmental Farm, where they used to test cattle feeds.

Farmworkers tell how 'Animal Liberationists' raided the farm, back in the 1980s, misunderstanding the innocuous nature of their work.

3. Follow the Sandstone Trail markers, to the right, on downhill between the sheds. Remember, this is a working farm: watch out for tractors and other agricultural machinery in the yard.

*Now preserved in the British Museum in London, the Malpas
Diploma was found close to the Barhill Downfall at Tushingham
in 1812*

Emerging from the farmyard, the limestone hardcore-surfaced
track curves northwards. At the bottom, another stile, next to
the middle of the three gates, takes the path on uphill, alongside
the hedge; and we cross the Tushingham-cum-Grindley parish
boundary.

*Tall thistles and poisonous foxgloves (from which a powerful heart
drug is made) splash the hedge with purple. Here the path goes under
an unsightly power line that marches off to the west.*

*According to a local farm worker, the so-called Roman Malpas
Diploma was found just beyond the first modern pylon in Bickley
Field—the field over the hedge to the left—in 1812. The bronze diploma,
or military discharge certificate, is now preserved in the British*

Museum, in London; though a copy can be seen in the Grosvenor Museum, Chester. Such certificates were issued to auxiliary soldiers of the Roman army on completion of 25 years service and granted them and their descendants citizenship and legalised their unofficial marriages. Like other diplomas from Britain and abroad, it tells us where different army units were stationed at different periods.

The Malpas Diploma was issued to a man called Reburrus, a junior cavalry officer—or decurio, *of the First Pannonian Regiment from Spain, on the 19th of January, AD 103. The two bronze plates, each about 9 by 6 inches/23 by 15 centimetres, are hinged together by bronze rings. There is no evidence so far of a settlement in the area, and it seems likely the diploma was lost as Reburrus travelled north on a minor Roman civil road that hugged the higher ground from* Mediolanum, *or Whitchurch, in Shropshire, 2 miles/3 kilometres away.*

Under a big oak at the top of the field, go left over a stile. Thirty metres on, the broad farm track continues through a metal kissing gate and rises diagonally to the right over rough pasture.

Look back to your left. Two fields away, among a group of trees, is Barhill Fall—a reputedly bottomless pit. A contemporary account tells how, back in 1687, a farmer travelling slowly along the old cart road (itself following a far older route) to church at St. Chad's Chapel was terrified by a 'huge noise' behind him. Turning round, he saw that a small hillock had disappeared into the earth, leaving a yawning hole. The culprit was an underground stream that had eaten away at a vast saltbed, causing the land above to cave in. But imagine the farmer's ignorant terror; as hell gaped he must have feared that demons would swirl up out of the pit, and that his end had come.

A tall Sandstone Trail marker post leads to another stile in the far, dog-legged corner of the field. From here, go left and over another stile, then follow the Sandstone Trail waymarkers towards the left-hand side of the large Victorian Bickley Hall Farm. Black and white Friesian cows dot the nearby pasture, their udders distended with milk. In summer scores of twittering house martins twist about the red brick barns; and sheep stare vacantly from the shade.

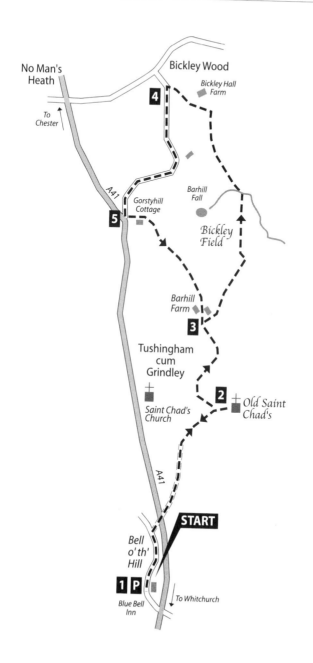

No Man's Heath

Bickley Wood

Bickley Hall Farm

To Chester

4

A41

Barhill Fall

Gorstyhill Cottage

5

Bickley Field

Barhill Farm

3

Tushingham cum Grindley

Saint Chad's Church

2 Old Saint Chad's

A41

START

Bell o' th' Hill

1 **P**

Blue Bell Inn

To Whitchurch

4. At the top of the slope, beyond the farm, the footpath crosses a stile and turns left to open onto a narrow country road. But while the Sandstone Trail goes off to the right, we turn left, back towards Bell o' the Hill.

Continue along the lane past Manor Farm.

5. Around ¹/₂ mile/0.75 kilometres later, turn left just before the junction with the old A41 at Gorstyhill Cottage. (The modern A41 rushes by a little further ahead). This little-used lane is a bridleway signposted to 'Willey Moor Lane'. It was originally a continuation of the sunken lane that leads from Bell o' th' Hill towards St Chad's chapel.

Go straight ahead, through the gate beside a small farm. A short section of green lane survives here beside an orchard. Over a stile, the path crosses a field—now with Barhill Fall among the trees to the left. The marshy hollow in the middle of the field here is supposedly where the Malpas Diploma was discovered.

Passing back under the power lines once more, the path continues over another stile and follows the field boundary, this time keeping the hedgerow on the right. The footpath emerges through a gate onto the farm track immediately below Barhill Farm.

Return uphill, through the farmyard, and turn immediately left over a stile. Now retrace your steps—via the field containing old St. Chad's Chapel—to the 'Blue Bell Inn' at Bell o' the' Hill and the end of the walk. Perhaps, if you're lucky, it may still be open.

10. Little Budworth

The Remains of Mondrum

Ancient commonland, sunken paths, mill pool, Romanies' meeting place, and the grave of the 'King of the Gypsies'

Start: *Little Budworth, 2 miles/3 kilometres west of Winsford. Near Oulton Park. Map reference: SJ 592654.*

Distance: *3 miles/5 kilometres.*

Duration: *Allow 2 hours.*

Difficulty: *Mostly flat; woodland paths, sandy tracks, field paths, quiet roadside. Usually dry, muddy in winter.*

Food and Drink: *The Red Lion, Vicarage Lane, Little Budworth. Cask ales. Homemade food, lunchtime and evenings. Beer garden. Children welcome. 01829 760275.*

Maps: *OS 1:25,000 Explorer 267 Northwich and Delamere Forest; OS 1:50,000 Landranger 117 Chester, Wrexham and surrounding area.*

FOUR FORESTS COVERED MUCH OF CHESHIRE in the time of the Norman Domesday Book. Wirral Forest to the west had been mainly cleared. Otherwise, apart from the as yet still sparsely inhabited Dee and Weaver valleys, most of the county was wild and wooded. Primeval Macclesfield Forest clothed the Pennines' eastern slopes. While a large part of central Cheshire, between the Mersey on the north and the Gowy and Weaver rivers to the west and east, formed the two forests of *Mara*—now Delamere— and *Mondrum*.

But they weren't forests in the way we think of them today; there were no dark ranks of Forestry Commission conifers, and even the original mixed oak woodlands were patchy, with large areas of open lowland heath dotted with boggy pools and meres.

'Forest' was no more than a legal term; and forests were simply wastelands ruled over by harsh laws that protected them for the hunting of a privileged few.

Nor were the ancient forests as tame and homogenised as modern Delamere. Wolf packs hunted among the trees as late as the 14th century. Both red and fallow deer browsed *Mara* and *Mondrum* until they were hunted out in the 17th century, during the Civil War. And among the recorded perks of a forester granted land at Little Budworth in 1153, were the rights to *'all sparrowhawks, merlins, hobbys, and swarms of bees'.* Rare birds indeed.

Little Budworth was part of *Mondrum.* Until the 1800s it was called Budworth-le-Frith—from a Welsh word *ffridd*, meaning something like 'upland common brought under cultivation'; and in 1650, nearby Oulton was also known as *Ferneleghes*, or the 'ferny clearings'. Forest clearance and settlement continued throughout the Middle Ages until, by the 17th century, *Mondrum* was no longer forest. Only one last vestige remained, unclaimed, unfarmed, and unbuilt upon; the poorest and most worthless part, a wasteland: Little Budworth Common. It was the last remains of *Mondrum.*

The walk

The walk begins outside the charming village of Little Budworth, close to Oulton Park motor-racing circuit, and just off the A49 Warrington-Whitchurch road. Follow the signs for Oulton Park. A car park at the southern end of the old Coach Road that cuts across Little Budworth Common, near the imposing Georgian gatehouse to Oulton Park, provides toilets and an information board. A sign on a bank announces that this is 'Little Budworth Country Park'.

1. From the car park, go through a narrow gap in the fence, on the opposite side of the car park to the toilets, and walk past the large sculptured chair.

Birches, gangling oaks, ferns and the whippy canes of wild raspberries rim the winding path. This is poor soil, almost pure sand—

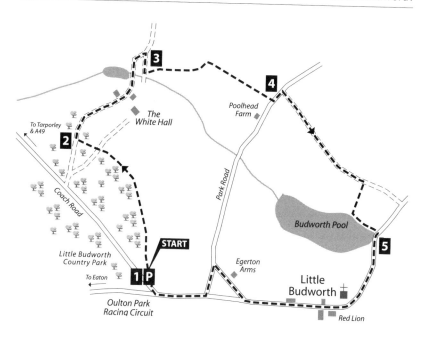

a legacy of the last Ice Age—overlain by a thin layer of leaf mould; and the barley fields beyond the trees to the right must rely largely on artificial fertilisers to grow at all.

The path runs parallel to fields on the right, eventually passing through a large gate across the path.

Nearby, an area of cleared birch scrub on the left, has been reclaimed by purple, honey-scented heather and ling, interspersed with splashes of yellow gorse. Harebells and yellow-petalled tormentil grow in the open patches; with foxgloves, honeysuckle and wood sage under the damper edges. The woods are good for fungi in the autumn, too. In addition to the ubiquitous wrens, chaffinches and tits, less common birds favour this unusual habitat: such as woodcock, redpolls and tree pipits. Little Budworth Common is one of the best surviving examples of lowland heath in Cheshire; larger, more typical open sandy areas can be seen on the other side of the Coach Road.

A hundred metres on, the path crosses a wider, metalled track.

Through stately wrought-iron gates a short distance off to the right, an avenue of tall limes dignifies black-and-white White Hall. It's the former home of the Earls of Shrewsbury who, along with the Egertons of Oulton Park, were local landowners.

2. Go straight on across the track. A hundred metres further on, at a crossing track, go right. Beyond White Hall the track narrows to a sandy path that dips between deep banks overhung with sycamores.

There are ferns along the banks and birdsong in the hedgerows. This is a Cheshire from before the First World War; a countryside of horses and narrow, unsurfaced lanes. And when an ivy-clad cottage looms between dense hedges on the bank above, the image seems confirmed.

Soon we cross a hollow where watercress grows in profusion in a boggy stream and there is a pool on the left.

The watercress was once exported in green bunches as far as London, but don't eat it now for fear of liver fluke. We shall meet the same stream later, on its downhill course to Budworth Pool.

Immediately after the hollow is a path junction. A track curves off to the left and a path leads right, beside the stream, but we go straight on, uphill along a section of sunken lane.

All these paths are old. The network of tracks and paths, both here and across the Common, are a reminder of the ancient open field and strip system, whereby land was shared out evenly. But by the 19th century, leasehold and freehold tenure had mostly overtaken the old medieval system. Fewer men were farming, now as tenants; and though the largest farms in Little Budworth were still only 109 and 199 acres, the size of farms was steadily growing. The 1839 Tithe map completes the picture of a small group of prosperous tenants and owner-occupiers. The countryside was changing; and the ordinary people of Little Budworth were getting poorer.

3. At the top of the slope the track runs on, soon passing houses but we go sharply to the right, back downhill, around a dogleg overgrown with wild broom, and into an even deeper, narrower sunken path. Don't miss this important turning.

Blackberry shoots reach out over the oak and hazel-lined path. Worn down by feet and hooves over the centuries, this sloping runnel of a path seems like a deep, green crevice in the sandy soil.

At the bottom of the slope, the path opens out immediately before a stream. Climb over a stile here and turn left, along the fence. Climb over a second stile into a field.

Turn right along the fence with the stream below. In the far corner of the field, cross another stile and follow a short section of path between hedges. Cross a stile before a house, and bear right, alongside the hedge.

These modern fields are an amalgam of several smaller pastures shown on early 19th century maps.

Go straight ahead, across a large open field towards a gate to the left of Poolhead Farm. Then turn left, out onto Park Road.

4. Within 50 metres, turn off Park Road to the right, and go down a broad green lane.

This was part of the old cattle drovers' road between Oswestry and Helsby. In the 18th century nearby 'Beggar's Bank' was a famous rendezvous for travelling people. The abundance in the area of such green lanes made Little Budworth Common a favourite atchin-tans *or stopping place for the 'dukes of little Egypt'.*

The common was somewhere they could park their vardos, *or covered wagons, and relax among their own people. For, until 1784 it was a criminal offence merely to be a gypsy, and in earlier days many were summarily executed. Imagine the tang of wood-smoke from their campfires hanging in the air, their cooking pots, lurcher dogs, grazing ponies, barefoot children, and bright washing draped across the bushes.*

The green lane runs on beneath tall ash trees, and drops downhill towards Budworth Pool. When the path levels out, ¼ mile/0.5 kilometre later, climb over a stile to the right, signposted for 'Budworth Mere'. Pass through a horse paddock to a stile beside the pool. Turn left along a path that runs beside the reed-fringed lake shore.

From medieval times Budworth Pool was important for its fish; but

Saint Peter's Church, Little Budworth

SAINT PETER'S CHURCH belonged originally to the nunnery of St Mary's in Chester. The oldest part is the simple stone tower in Perpendicular style, with its carved faces and gargoyles. Built sometime between 1490 and 1526, the church dates from the late Middle Ages. Until early this century there was an iron brazier mounted on the roof that held a beacon for signalling in times of war.

In 1757 the church was described as *'a neat building of red stone, having a tower at the west end, with two side aisles supported by wooden pillars'*. The body of the church was rebuilt in stone in 1800 in Georgian style, using huge blocks of stone 6 feet/2 metres long; and was paid for by the wealthy merchant son of a local farmer.

Inside the church are a Georgian pulpit and a fine 17th century fluted font, carved from fossil marble. The rest of the old fittings were lost in the 1870 'restoration'.

More interesting, perhaps, is an account of 1757 that tells us, *'The churchyard of Little Budworth in Cheshire contains the grave of one who in his day and generation was 'King of the Gypsies'. This person, Henry Lovett, died in 1745 at the age of 85.'* He died a protestant and is buried, so an even older account tells us, *'On the north side of the Church Yard, by the Rails of it, opposite the Chancel, where lies a large Stone upon the Ground.'*

today Tarporley Angling Club fish for sport, not food. In around 1300, it was called Walkemulnepoul *meaning 'watermill pool'. Beyond a stile, beneath tall willows on the opposite side of the road is what was, until the end off the 19th century, the old water-powered flourmill, now converted into an attractive home.*

5. Turn right, up Mill Lane. At the top of the hill go right again, around the bend, and into Little Budworth village.

Until quite recently, only a few thatched cottages clung to the skirts of the church, perched on its rock outcrop above the mere. In 1841 there were only 74 houses and 330 people in the parish; two tailors, a shoemaker and a blacksmith. Opposite the Red Lion, which dates back to the 1700s, is the church of St. Peter, reached by a fine set of stone steps.

From the church, continue through the village, past the 'Old Vicarage' until, ¹/₂ mile/1 kilometre later you come to the almshouses on the corner of Pinfold Lane. Built in 1740, they gave a home to *'Six poor men and six poor women of the parish, with free medicine and coal, and an extra half crown at Christmas'.*

Go right at the war memorial to the fallen of the 'Great War of 1914-19', down Pinfold Lane. Close by is the attractive Egerton Arms, a free house, next door to 'Oulton Park Cricket Club'.

At the junction of Pinfold and Park Lanes, is the old pinfold. A

The churchyard of St Peter's Church, Little Budworth, contains the grave of Henry Lovatt, the 'king of the gypsies', who died on Little Budworth Common in 1745

plaque on the wall inside tells us that it is 'an enclosure in which stray animals were impounded until claimed on the payment of a fine, which has existed on this site since the 17th century. Restored and repaired 1986.' *Which brings to mind the story from elsewhere in Cheshire, of the squatter who, building a roof and chimney on a pinfold between sunset and sunrise, was able to claim it as his home.*

From the pinfold, turn sharp left along the lane. At the junction, 50 metres on, go right, away from the village, towards Oulton Park.

Over the hedge to the right is the village football field, which slopes alarmingly into the wheat field beyond.

A hundred metres further on are the beech-tree shaded ornamental gates to Oulton Park, designed by Vanburgh.

Now a famous motor-racing circuit, Oulton Park was the former stately home of the Egertons, a prominent Cheshire family. Oulton Hall burned down twice, once in 1720 and again in 1926. Strangely, the ruins were later bombed in 1940, during the Second World War. The park, laid out by William Eames, a famous landscape gardener of his day, once contained a herd of 300 deer. The hall and grounds were taken over by the army during the Second World War, when it became the headquarters of the American General Patton as he prepared for the D-Day invasion of Europe.

Opposite the gates, turn right, back down the old Coach Road, which was built in about 1740 as a drive to Oulton Hall. A hundred metres later, turn back into the car park and the end of the walk.

We've come full circuit: from cars to foot, horseback, cart and gypsy caravan, and back to cars again.

11. Whitegate

Where Vale Royal Abbey stood

Picturesque village, Nun's Grave and ghost, site of Vale Royal Abbey, wooded Weaver Valley, and prophesies of Nixon—the Cheshire seer

Start: *Whitegate, 5 miles/8 kilometres south-west of Northwich. Map reference: SJ 629694*

Distance: *3 miles/5 kilometres.*

Duration: *Allow 3 hours.*

Difficulty: *Mostly flat; drive, wooded farmland, sandy paths and riverbank. Muddy in places.*

Food and Drink: *The Plough Inn, Beauty Bank, Whitegate. Greenall Whitley. Bar snacks and food. 01606 889455.*

Maps: *OS 1:25,000 Explorer 267 Northwich and Delamere Forest; OS 1:50,000 Landranger 118 Stoke-on-Trent and Macclesfield area.*

A KING'S VOW TO THE VIRGIN MARY marked the start of the as yet unfinished story of Vale Royal. As a young prince returning from crusade in the Holy Land, during the winter of 1263-4, King Edward I was caught in a violent storm in the Bay of Biscay. *'Hear me, oh Blessed Virgin,'* he promised, *'and, in humble gratitude, I shall build a convent for a hundred monks of the order of Cistercians.'* It seems his prayers were answered. For, as he struggled ashore, the last to land, he looked back in time to see his ship vanish beneath the crashing surf. Only two men survived. It was an experience strong enough to bind any prince of Christendom to his vow.

But the implementation of his solemn promise was delayed. For no sooner had he escaped with his life than the Barons' Wars began, and both King Henry and the Prince were held prisoner by Simon de Montfort. Only when he became king, five years later, was Edward (who was known as 'longshanks' because of his unusual height) able to found his new abbey. As Royal Earl of Cheshire, he chose initially a site at Darnhall in Delamere Forest. Later it was moved to Whitegate, above the River Weaver. Edward I called it the Vale Royal, and decreed, *'there shall be no monastery more royal than this one, in liberties, wealth and honour, throughout the whole world.'*

Whitegate is named after the white gates that once led up to the abbey. Clustered around the village green are the church, school and two thatched black-and-white cottages, one of which dates from 1656. They nestle in a hollow among pools and tall trees, to form a perfect scene.

A medieval wooden church built on this site in the 14th century by the monks of Vale Royal Abbey was rebuilt twice, in 1728 and again in 1874. Today, a half-timbered porch leads to a heavily studded door dating back to the 18th century; while inside there is a splendid hammer-beam roof supported by eight original medieval pillars. Outside, a squat, shingled spire looks down through wrought-iron gates to the village green, the scene of today's Whitsun Fair maypole dances.

Across the green is stately Whitegate House, a 17th century building that was once an inn called The Rifleman. A rent book for 1853 records that the licensee was paid for 30 dinners at 1s 6d, 24 quarts of ale at 8d, and 43 pints at 4d—a lot of money in those days! Even so, the pub lost its licence in 1870 because Lady Delamere, the wife of the owner of Vale Royal House, objected to *'the unseemly behaviour of customers on the green.'*

The walk

1. The walk begins in the centre of Whitegate, close to St Mary's Church. Park close to the gates and sandstone lodge at the start of the old drive to Vale Royal House. Flanked by an avenue of tall beeches and limes, the drive leads gently uphill past residential houses on Sutton Field road, and on towards Vale Royal House.

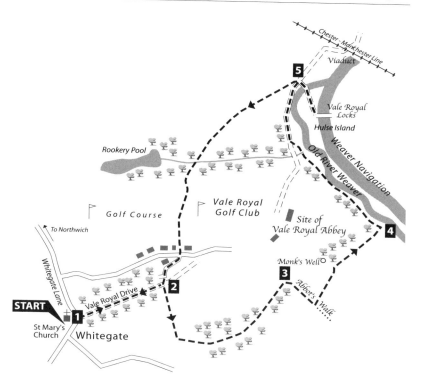

Within 200 metres, a metal gate blocks the drive. A sign announces; 'No Through Road. Use St Mary's Drive for Vale Royal Drive'. When new luxury houses and a landscaped 18 hole golf course were built to the left of the drive, through the trees, in the 1990s, the old drive was closed to traffic.

2. A quarter of a mile/0.5 kilometre later, with new houses visible on the left, turn right on a cross path marked by a fingerpost with white walking figures on a green background. Go over a stile and head straight across the field, towards the woods.

At the far side of the field, enter the wood. Go through the gap beside the field gate and follow the footpath as it curves to the left beneath the trees.

The floor of this mixed deciduous wood is open and sunny, and sweet with the scent of bluebells in early summer.

Vale Royal House stands on the site of the vast but unfinished medieval Vale Royal Abbey. Parts of the original monastic buliding are reputed to survive in the cellars

When the path splits, keep to the main, right-hand path. Follow the path straight ahead, through the woods. The woodland narrows, and the path runs on beneath tall beeches.

At the end of the strip of trees, cross a simple footbridge made of railway sleepers.

Ahead, select homes sit amid mown pastures in the old grounds of Vale Royal House.

3. Turn right, along the woodland edge.

For a while the path follows the old Abbot's Walk, marked on early maps. Behind us and to the left, the clock tower of Vale Royal House is just visible, peeping above tennis courts.

A hundred metres or so later, turn left over a ladder stile. From here a short permissive path veers to the right and cuts obliquely across the corner of the pasture. Climb over a second ladder stile,

Vale Royal Abbey and House

IN ITS PRIME Vale Royal was the largest Cistercian Abbey in England. The foundation stone for the high altar was laid by Edward l in 1277 at a ceremony attended by barons, bishops and all the trappings of Plantagenet power. At the feast afterwards they ate roast porpoises.

Endowments of land between Winsford and Frodsham were made to support the Abbey; and over £38,000 in the money of the time—a vast sum—was spent on its construction over the next 50 years. But Edward's incessant wars drained the coffers, and by 1336, in the reign of his grandson, the walls of the church were still unroofed.

For a while the Black Prince breathed new life into the project, but in October 1360 a storm blew down the entire nave, and at the Prince's death in 1376, royal patronage ended. If it had been finished, the church would have been both bigger and longer than Fountains Abbey, in Yorkshire.

After Henry VIII's Dissolution of the monasteries in 1539, the monks were turfed out and the property and land sold to Sir John Holcroft of Lancashire. Much of the Abbey was demolished; but substantial parts of the monks' quarters were incorporated into later buildings, and still exist, particularly in the cellars.

Two generations later the Cholmondeleys, a Cheshire family, bought Vale Royal; and here they entertained King James l in 1617 on his celebrated visit to the Cheshire salt mines. But soon afterwards, during the Civil War, Parliamentary forces sacked the house and burnt down part of one wing.

Archaeological excavations in 1911-12 and 1958 established the plan of the church laid out in 1278. Basically cruciform, it had a central tower and two smaller towers above the west end, with cloisters on the south side of the nave. The site of the Nun's Grave—from which a ghost allegedly still walks today—marks the east end where the high altar once stood.

go through the hedge, and turn immediately left along the field boundary.

Within 200 metres, continue ahead through a gap in the hedge.

The dense woods to the left are part of the now overgrown ornamental gardens of Vale Royal House, and the site of the Victorian pheasantry and the far older Monks' Well.

The path follows the field boundary for 30 metres or so, then kinks half right across the centre of the field, following a line of oaks that mark the line of the old hedgerow between what was once two fields.

4. At the bottom of the undulating field, the path enters the trees again. Beyond the stile, turn left and follow a clear path along the sloping bank beside the woodland edge.

To the right of the path, the wetter ground that slopes down to a loop of the old, uncanalised river, is rank with nettles and clad in hazel, elder and rowan.

Soon the path drops diagonally down a slope between dark rhododendrons.

Glimpses of the placid water below show fishermen lining the banks in season, waiting patiently to catch big carp, bream and tench. It's an idyllic spot, but the overhanging trees mean there are no anglers on this side.

The path crosses a silted up brook full of black leaf-mould.

Water dribbles over a curved, brick-built weir into the river. Its ceaseless trickle echoes under the dank trees.

Beyond the splashing stream, the path continues through the woods.

Up to the left, where wild daffodils once grew, are the mown greens and fairways of Vale Royal Abbey Golf Club. The gothic roofs and chimneys of Vale Royal House loom above the lip of the slope.

Nixon, the Cheshire prophet, is said to have been born in Whitegate in 1467. A simple ploughboy, he is credited with some extraordinary prophesies which were made when he fell into one of his regular trances. Among them, he foretold that Vale Royal Abbey would become a ravens'

39 Vale Royal Locks, near Northwich

Peaceful Vale Royal Locks, on the River Weaver near Hartford, has changed surprisingly little since this old postcard was published in the early 1900s

nest; and it is true that in 1538 the estate was bought by the Holcrofts—whose crest was a raven!

The path continues through the woods, now with the old river immediately below.

Kingfishers nest nearby and the river margin is lush with yellow flag and watercress.

Over a stile, the path winds down to the water's edge, where thickets of head-high rosebay willow herb stretch away on either side.

Four hundred metres later, when the path emerges onto Vale Royal Drive—which, though private, is also a public right of way in parts—go right, along the tarmaced drive.

5. Five hundred metres later, leave the drive and turn right onto a track that crosses the old arm of the Weaver on a black and white, cast iron bridge. You are now on Hulse's Island.

This charming, wooded part of the Weaver Valley sees hundreds of anglers at weekends immersed in silent concentration. Downriver a flotilla of swans drifts under the viaduct of the Chester to Manchester railway line.

Continue along the track until you come to Vale Royal Locks, part of the Weaver Navigation.

Brine springs on the Weaver's banks upstream attracted the Romans, and by 1732 over 9,000 tons of rock salt and 5,000 tons of white salt were carried downstream annually. After several attempts, an Act of Parliament to canalise the river was passed; and in 1830 it was dredged to a depth of 7' 6"/2.5 metres, while locks 88 feet/28 metres long were built to allow cargoes of up to 150 tonnes to be carried. The locks were widened to 42 feet/13 metres in 1874. The last large ship passed through Vale Royal Locks in 1969.

Return over the arm of the old river to Vale Royal Drive and go back to the left, under dark, overhanging yews and hollies. Within 35 metres, bear right up a clearly waymarked flight of shallow sandstone steps bordered by dense rhododendrons. At the top of the short slope, a wooden gate leads out into open fields. Ahead, the path snakes diagonally across undulating pasture to a distant line of trees.

At the woodland edge, a quarter of a mile/0.5 kilometre later, go through a kissing gate and descend steps into the shade of the trees. Turn half right, and follow the path over a wooden footbridge.

Ignore the signed footpath on the right before the bridge; it points to Rookery Pool: a 5 acre/2 hectare fishing water that once featured a boathouse belonging to Vale Royal House.

These lovely open, deciduous woods are home to a wealth of birds and animals. Across the stream, the path winds through groves of mature beeches heavy with the scent of bluebells in early summer. Fallen trees, dips and hillocks add to the appeal of the place.

At the far edge of this narrow finger of woodland, the path crosses Vale Royal Abbey Golf Club's course.

Once part of nearby Poolfields Farm, the course was constructed

*on rich farmland in the 1990s. The old barley, potato and sugar beet
fields are now manicured fairways. Every hillock, copse and pond is
new.*

Follow the waymarkers to the left, and then curve right to
meet a gravel path. Continue straight ahead, passing a reeded
artificial lake on your right.

*Across the course, a line of large modern houses lines the old drive.
To the left is elegant Vale Royal House.*

Beyond the 18th tee, the public right of way continues through
a kissing gate and on between the houses. Fifty metres later, the
path emerges on a road with a sign for 'St Mary's Drive' directly
opposite.

Cross over and walk along St Mary's Drive. At the end, a path
leads back to Vale Royal Drive hidden beneath its avenue of lofty
beeches. Turn right, along the drive, and return to St Mary's
Church to complete the walk.

*An oasis of green between Winsford and Northwich, Whitegate with
its black and white cottages, its church, its maypole, its trees, its pools,
parkland and river valley is still aptly named: it is still a 'Vale Royal of
England'. And despite the inevitable pressures for change, let us hope
it stays that way.*

12. Lindow Moss

In Search of the Bog Man

Lindow Common and Black Lake, Lindow Moss, peat cutters, and two 'bog burials'—Iron Age sacrificial victims preserved in the peat

Start: *Wilmslow, 10 miles/16 kilometres south of Manchester. Map reference SJ 833814.*

Distance: *3¹/₂ miles/5.5 kilometres.*

Duration: *Allow 2¹/₂-3 hours.*

Difficulty: *Flat. Surfaced paths, lanes, sandy bridleways, peat bog and mossland. Wet and muddy in winter. Potentially dangerous for children and dogs.*

Food and Drink: *Boddington Arms Pub and Restaurant, Altrincham Road, Wilmslow, opposite the car park at the northern end of Lindow Common. Garden. Children welcome. 01625 525849.*

Maps: *OS 1:25,000 Explorer 268, Wilmslow, Macclesfield and Congleton; OS 1:50,000 Landranger 118 Stoke-on-Trent and Macclesfield area.*

LINDOW MOSS IS A SINISTER PLACE. Dark forces lurk there still. Cross the bog on a winter's day scoured by horizontal rain, and the morass of peat diggings, black-water ditches, birch scrub and heathland evokes a distant past inhabited by earth deities, water spirits and the supernatural.

Even today Cheshire is rich in Celtic tradition: 'horsing' and 'soul-caking' are practised annually at Antrobus, sword and antler dances have their followers, stone heads are venerated yet. While the 'Old Religion' lives on, the sophistication of the Electronic Age remains a thin veneer. And, as if to remind us of the proximity of this alien past, the naturally embalmed body of an Iron Age sacrificial victim was unearthed from the Moss in

August 1984. Pickled by the peat, he was called the 'Bog Man' by archaeologists; while some wit from the press dubbed him 'Pete Marsh'.

Meres, marshes and mosslands once covered large tracts of Cheshire. Little now remains, and that only in fragments. Lindow Moss was formed in two shallow hollows within the boulder clay and glacial gravels left behind after the last Ice Age. Originally it extended over 1,500 acres/600 hectares in the shape of a ragged tea cosy. But by the 1840s the Moss had shrunk to only 750 acres/300 hectares, and today it covers only about 80 acres/32 hectares, half of which is now worked commercially for peat extraction.

The walk

Our walk begins on the eastern outskirts of Wilmslow, 10 miles/ 16 kilometres south of Manchester city centre, at the northern tip of Lindow Common. Turn off the A538 Wilmslow-Altrincham

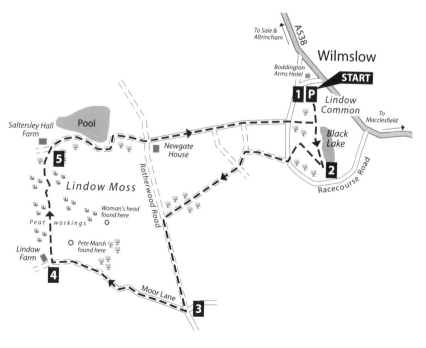

road by the Boddington Arms Pub and Restaurant, onto Racecourse Road. The road circles the Common. The large public car park opposite the pub has ample parking space and leads straight out onto the Common.

1. Go through the wooden gate at the far end of the car park.

A Borough of Macclesfield and English Nature interpretation board here explains the importance and management of Lindow Common. Its main significance is the internationally recognised importance of lowland heath. Lindow Common is one of only a few areas of this threatened habitat in Cheshire and is now protected as both a Local Nature Reserve and Site of Special Scientific Interest (SSSI).

Careful management helps ensure the survival here of rare animals and plants such as so-called common lizards and common frogs, newts, butterflies, dragonflies, round-leaved sundew, bog asphodel, cranberry and cotton grass.

Out on the Common a web of paths spreads through the mixed birch, willow and heather scrub.

At the first junction of paths, within 100 metres of the gate, continue straight ahead on a grassy path that runs out onto the open heath. The paths cuts through a narrow band of trees to emerge at Black Lake.

It's from this oval lake at the heart of the Common that Lindow gets its name. Back in the Iron Age this part of Cheshire was still under Celtic control; the two Celtic Welsh words llyn *and* ddu *mean 'lake' and 'black' respectively. Lindow is the* black lake.

The Common was once part of an originally far larger Lindow Moss. Pollen samples from peat deposited nearly two thousand years ago show that by late Roman times the woodland on the edge of the Moss had been cleared, and the area was a mixture of wasteland and pasture. And like 'wasteland' today, the Moss became a place on the margins of society, a place for the poor, the dispossessed, and the outcast.

During the 1700s a shepherd became a well-known figure on the Common; he carried a crook and wore low shoes with large buckles, knee breeches, a red waistcoat, a brown topcoat and a round hat.

Local children larking about on the ice on Lindow Common's Black Lake around 1910. Notice their bicycles propped against a tree on the island

In about 1771, Squire Finney, a local landowner and magistrate, persuaded two local lords to enclose much of the Moss; ironically, part of the rents raised was used to build a workhouse for the poor on the edge of the Common in 1773. Later the open ground on the Common was used for horseracing.

But disastrous fires often swept the Common in dry summers, and a photograph from the 1890s shows the area as a sandy, treeless heath. Adders up to 14 inches/35 centimetres long were common and a viper catcher came to trap them each year; in 1877 a boy was bitten whilst collecting bilberries. Finally, in 1897 the Common was bought for a large sum by a local J.P., and presented to Wilmslow District Council on Queen Victoria's Diamond Jubilee.

At the Black Lake turn right on the broad, encircling path.

Today, a simple wire fence encircles the lake to protect the fragile wildlife habitat around the margin. Mixed flocks of ducks and gulls sit in rafts out on the dark water. But if the heather and birch scrub evoke the distant past, the roar of passenger jets taxiing for take-off at nearby Manchester Airport is a salutary reminder of the present.

2. Beyond the last seat and immediately before the end of the lake, take the path that doubles back sharply to the right.

Twenty metres later, continue on across a minor path. Our path veers to the right and then runs on straight across the open heathland. At the next junction of paths, 100 metres on, turn left towards the edge of the Common. Go through the wooden kissing gate and cross Racecourse Road.

Directly opposite is Lindow Lane—marked by a sign with white letters on a green ground. This is the old margin of the Moss. Ignore a signposted bridleway running off to the left and carry on down Lindow Lane.

Now ponies of the rich graze on either side; but once the Moss was the last resort of the poor, where ordinary people had cut turves for the fire, collected firewood and grazed cows, pigs and ponies since time immemorial.

Within 250 metres of the road, by cream-painted Racecourse Farm, the potholed lane bends sharply to the left. The narrow lane bends to the right again and runs out across the Moss, past paddocks and ramshackle stables, and on beneath a natural avenue of birch and young ash trees.

There is scrub woodland to the left. Notice how the path is raised above the surrounding land; drained for a century and more, the Moss is drying out, shrinking, and settling back upon itself.

When the rough limestone surfaced lane bends sharply to the left, go straight on, on a narrow but well-used bridleway beneath a green tunnel of trees. Another 200 metres on, at a T-junction of paths, turn left onto a broad bridleway, called Rotherwood Road. Alder and sycamore fringe the path, now raised more obviously above the fields.

Beyond a couple of secluded houses, the bridleway is tarmaced. At the end of this metalled section two County Council signs, on the left, tell us this is 'Public Path 34' and the 'Bridle Path To Morley'. Continue on past Springfield Drive to the end of Rotherwood Road.

3. Then turn right, along Moor Lane, keeping an eye out for traffic. Continue past 'Ned Yates' Garden Centre'. From here a patchy tarmac road winds out past several houses into open farmland. When the road forks, continue along the lane to the right. Soon the lane passes 'Wilmslow Peat Farm' and 'Foxholme Stables'.

At the end of a straight stretch of road the lane bends sharply to the left. Around the corner is the entrance to 'Lindow Court Park' caravan site, while ahead are the orange, metal gates of 'Horticon Ltd'. Turn right on the signposted public path between the two. Overshadowed by tall trees and the hedge, the path runs alongside the caravan park.

4. Less than 100 metres from the lane, turn right, through a gap in the fence between two posts. The turning is easy to miss; look out for a post bearing a yellow footpath arrow waymarker in the hedgerow on the left. The path cuts across a field and tarmac drive to a metal kissing gate on the far side. Beyond the gate, a crude concrete slab bridges a ditch cut deep into the black peat.

From here the path heads out across the Moss. Suddenly, we've stepped into a different world.

Out to the left, a deep drainage ditch filled with black water hints at the depth of the peat. Beyond, the Moss is blanketed in open heather dotted with sparse birch and patches of white cotton grass. The sheer extent of the Moss in the past slowly becomes apparent. In the last century both men and cattle were drowned in the bog, which was far wetter then. Though partially drained today, these peat workings remain treacherous; dogs still drown in the vertically sided ditches, and the solid appearance of the cut peat surface is often deceptive— step off the path and you could sink up to your waist, or worse. Be warned!

Lindow Woman
And Lindow Man:
The Bodies In The Bog

IN MAY 1983 two workmen discovered a round, peat covered object at the peat-packing plant on the edge of the Moss. It was soft and pliable and, as a joke, they called it a dinosaur's egg. But when they hosed it clean they saw it was a human skull, with traces of hair and flesh still attached.

The police were promptly called. A local man subsequently panicked and confessed to the murder of his wife; and was later tried and convicted.

Yet, in a cruel twist of fate, the skull turned out to belong not to his wife's body, but to a woman who had died 2,500 years earlier, around 500 BC, back in the Iron Age.

Despite careful searches, no other trace of the corpse was found; it seems likely that the head alone was buried in the bog as part of a Celtic ritual sacrifice.

A year later one of the same workmen pulled a well-preserved leg from the peat elevator. When archaeologists visited the Moss the next morning they discovered a flap of skin protruding from the uncut edge of the peat, not far from the site where the woman's skull had been buried.

On excavation it turned out to be the ancient body of an Iron Age man pickled in the peat.

The lower half of the body was missing, cut off by the mechanical diggers. Tests showed the dead man had been about 25 years old, was fit and that his teeth were in good condition. He had a well-trimmed beard and moustache, and his manicured nails suggest he was probably a nobleman.

That this was a ritual killing is supported by his wounds. There was damage to the skull, around the neck was a twisted leather thong, and the throat had been slit; Lindow Man was first knocked unconscious, then slowly garotted, and lastly had his throat cut. In his preserved stomach were found traces of burnt bread and mistletoe, sacred to the Druids.

It seems probable that he suffered the 'threefold death' referred to by the Roman chronicler, Lucan, as a sacrifice to a triad of powerful Celtic gods: *Teutates*, *Esus* and *Taranis*. The burnt bread and sacred mistletoe were his last meal.

Lindow Moss may have been a grisly Iron Age votive site, a place of great sanctity in an ancient water cult.

Other human remains from the Iron Age and Roman periods have also been found here. Parts of a second Iron Age man's body were unearthed in 1987. Remarkably, he had an extra thumb on his right hand. Was it this deformity that had marked him out for sacrifice?

Today, the twisted body of the first Lindow bog man is displayed in a case in the British Museum in London.

Perhaps in a reflection of our obsession with the grisly, the ancient corpse is said to be the museum's most popular exhibit.

Less well known and therefore less visited is the severed head of the so-called Lindow Woman. Her freeze-dried head stares blankly from its case.

But in a chilling twist to the tale, it has recently been suggested that the preserved head *actually* belongs not to some ancient victim, but to the local man's murdered wife…

Walk on between the scrubby birch trees that cling to the path edge. Soon the vast 'peat diggings' open out on either side.

Most of the cut peat is used as garden potting compost. Yet there are plenty of good alternatives, and groups such as The National Trust no longer use peat at all. It seems ironic that on tiny Lindow Common, English Nature are taking such pains to protect this 'rare and special habitat' *while nearby huge tracts of the Moss are being strip mined for a quick profit. Once gone, this internationally threatened habitat can never be replaced. The extraction of peat from Lindow Moss remains controversial and is opposed by many local people.*

On either side, black spires of drying peat are heaped across the Moss. The gnarled roots of ancient trees dragged from the peat pepper the surface like clawed hands. We are back in a landscape reminiscent of an older Cheshire, a landscape before forest clearance, agricultural drainage, and the patchwork of hedged fields that characterise the land today. Half close your eyes, and this last fragment of the Moss grows in the imagination: dotted in the distant past with reed-rimmed pools, it is larger, wetter, silent and more dangerous. Water rails scream in the reed-beds like stuck pigs. It is an eerie fastness filled with menace. And beneath the surface of the pools Celtic boggarts and bobodha— or bogey-men—wait to pull the careless wanderer down into the black water.

From the Bronze Age onwards, prehistoric man no doubt fished and hunted here for eels, otters and wild ducks. The Moss was rich with opportunity; a place to be exploited even then. A Victorian writer mentions 'what appeared to be a roadway made of logs of timber placed end to end, with sleepers across, laid close together, and this I am told continued for some length up the Moss'. *This sounds very much like the prehistoric 'Sweet Track' found in the Somerset Levels (a similar ancient wetland)—a primitive access road.*

Walk on. The peat diggings open out on either side.

Concealed beneath the dark surface here are often macabre relics of an unkind past. Bogs are peculiar in many ways. William King, the Archbishop of Dublin, wrote in 1685, 'that a Turf-Bog preserves things strangely, a Corps will ly entire in one for several years; I have seen a piece of leather pretty fresh dug out of a Turf-Bog, that had never in the memory of man been dug before.'

At Burwell Fen, in East Anglia, the preserved body of a man was found upright in the peat in the position in which he had drowned. Dressed in a belted leather coat, he stood in a wooden dugout canoe, his arm still raised in a last gesture of horror. He died perhaps 2,500 years ago, back in the Iron Age. Even more bizarre is the unauthenticated account of a knight in full armour, still mounted on his horse, found in Solway Moss where, centuries before, a battle was fought in 1542. Choked in a nightmare mixture of mud and water, both died in terror to be preserved inadvertently for posterity.

But not all bodies preserved in the peat have died a natural death. Some have been murdered, and others sacrificed in ritual killings. Two such victims have been found right here, beneath Lindow Moss.

Keep to the path. Soon two narrow bridges made of baulks of timber and steel plate cross parallel drainage ditches that run out into the Moss. Take care. The deep water is an inky black and the sides are sheer; to fall in might prove fatal.

Today, long-armed diggers excavate 200 metre long 'rooms' in the peat. Until the 1990s, a narrow gauge railway used to haul the half-dried peat to the processing depot snaked away from here across the peat. Yet for centuries the peat was cut by hand. In the past it was used as fuel, not wantonly for gardens and horticultural big business, and so was cut in 'turfs', or slabs. In the early 1900s one of the peat cutters was Old Jobie. He lived in a one-room shack out on the Moss, and could cut up to five thousand peats a week, for which he was paid £5.

Beyond the two bridges the path climbs into bracken and willow scrub. Veer left at the top of the slope, curve around to the right beneath the birch trees, and cross a further bridge to the left into a wood. On the far side of the bridge is a 'Private Nature Reserve' sign. Turn right and follow the path, beside the fence, through scrubby woodland.

The springy peat is replaced by sand underfoot, and we have temporarily left the Moss.

5. Roughly 300 metres later, climb over a stile, go up some steps, and turn right along a tarmaced lane away from Saltersley Farm.

Continue along the track. Beyond a collection of ramshackle lean-tos is Rossmere Lake.

It's a disused sandpit that has since filled with water. A story in the local press tells how, a number of years ago, a man returned from abroad to find his favourite footpath submerged by this new pool. So, in protest and to the loud cheers of a crowd of onlookers, he swam across the lake in a wetsuit and flippers to join up the severed ends of the path. No wonder he got his picture in the paper! Today the pool attracts keen fishermen from Macclesfield's 'Prince Albert Angling Society'. Bream, roach, rudd, perch and pike mingle with a few hefty carp—the largest caught here back in 1988 weighed 18lb/8 kilos.

The potholed track curves around the lake, and into the shade of scrubby birch, ash and oak woodland. Brick and wooden 'villas', shacks and bungalows here are the descendants of squatters' homes shown built on the same spot on the 1843 Tithe Map of the area.

A gypsy caravan, or vardo, *parked on the fringes of Black Lake on Lindow Common in the early 1900s*

Three hundred metres later, the track emerges on a metalled road. The bridle path to the right leads back to Moor Lane, but we turn right, along narrow Newgate Road, past a sign that warns, '!—*Animals. SLOW*'. Beyond 'Newgate Kennels and Cattery', on the left, is 'Newgate Disposal Site'. What appear to be undulating hills here are actually composed entirely of modern rubbish; this above ground landfill is yet another way in which the Moss is undervalued and abused. Perhaps 100 feet/30 metres below this modern waste is the deep black peat of the unwanted Moss—an older 'wasteland'.

From here Newgate Road runs directly back to Lindow Common. When the road meets Racecourse Road, cross carefully and go through the wooden kissing gate opposite, back onto the Common. Beyond the encircling strip of trees, continue straight ahead, across a major path, and then veer left, out over the grass and heather of the open heath.

Within 200 metres, turn left on a well used path; 100 metres on, bear right on another path beneath the trees. Follow the path to the left to emerge back at the car park opposite the Boddington Arms Pub and Restaurant.

After the brooding solitude and black foreboding of the Moss, Wilmslow's well-tended fringe seems almost tame. Yet, if the wild Moss should vanish altogether—under sprawling homes or ill-considered landfill—it seems likely there will be secrets hidden still within the depths, of ancient sacrifice, dark rites and death.

13. Alderley Edge

Across the Copper Hills

Legend of the Wizard of Alderley Edge, Bronze Age copper mines, Engine Vein, Stormy Point, Devil's Grave, Saddle Bole, Holy Well, Armada Beacon, Castle Rock, Wizard's Well, caves and hidden mine entrances

---

Start: *Alderley Edge, 12 miles/19 kilometres south of Manchester. National Trust car park, on the B5087. Map reference: SJ 860772.*

Distance: *3 miles/5 kilometres.*

Duration: *Allow 2 hours.*

Difficulty: *Fairly level, but with steep paths on slopes of Alderley Edge. Dry and sandy, muddy patches in winter.*

Food and Drink: *The Wizard of Edge restaurant, Macclesfield Road, Nether Alderley. Modern British food. Drinks only with food. 01625 584000. OR Wizard Tearoom (seasonal).*

Maps: *OS 1:25,000 Explorer 268 Wilmslow, Macclesfield and Congleton; OS 1:50,000 Landranger Sheet 118, Stoke-on-Trent and Macclesfield area.*

ONCE UPON A TIME, SO THE TRADITIONAL LEGEND OF ALDERLEY EDGE BEGINS, a Mobberley farmer, crossing the Edge on his way to market to sell a white mare, is accosted by a wizard. Appearing from nowhere, the old man tells the farmer:

"Thy horse is doomed to be,
Heir to a nobler destiny"

Puzzled, at first the farmer refuses to part with the horse. But on his return across the Edge, after a fruitless day at market, he readily agrees. The wizard leads the farmer, past a number of carefully mentioned places on the Edge, to the Iron Gates—a magical entrance to the underworld, concealed within the rock. There, deep in a cavern, he sees a circle of fully-armed warriors, each with a milk-white steed, lying in an enchanted sleep. They await some dark and future day when they will ride out to save all England. But one warrior lies next to an empty space—he has no horse. At last the farmer understands. And so, in return for the horse, the wizard pays the farmer three times the animal's value, in treasure from a subterranean store.

Treasure? A subterranean store? Yes, for hidden within the legend are clues to real events; events in a distant past that were to shape the face of Cheshire. Perhaps such clues are older folk memories woven into traditional story form. Whatever their origin, the list of places named in the legend helps to illuminate Man's earliest search for metals which began some 4,000 years ago, back in the Bronze Age. Copper ore has long been mined under the Edge. The old mine workings: levels, adits, spoil heaps,

Originally called the 'Miner's Arms', the old 'Wizard Inn' celebrated the well-known legend of Alderley Edge

smelting hearths and inclines can still be traced today. The wizard's real treasure was the copper concealed beneath Cheshire's sandstone hills!

The walk

The walk begins at the National Trust car park—just beyond The Wizard Country Restaurant, one mile/1.5 kilometres east of Alderley Edge on the B5087 Alderley Edge-Macclesfield road. There's plenty of parking space, toilets, and a picnic area; and sometimes even an ice-cream van.

1. From the car park, take the short path that leads to 'The Wizard of Edge' restaurant.

Originally a pub called the Miners Arms, it now has tearooms and a National Trust Information Room behind.

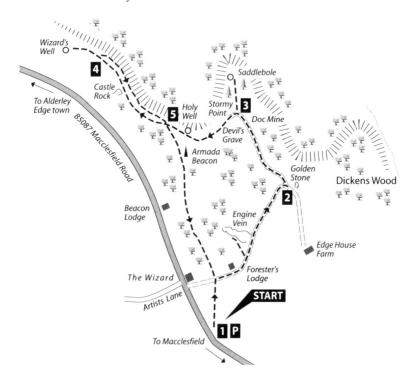

It's chastening to realise that Alderley Edge's beautiful woodland, paths and views, and all its priceless archaeological treasures were almost sold off to housing developers just before the Second World War. But for a twist of fate, all this would be buried under the villas of Manchester's mercantile princes and fêted footballers. Happily, 218 acres/90 hectares of the Edge were bought by the local Pilkington sisters with the help of Cheshire County Council in 1938, and later given to The National Trust for everyone to enjoy.

Turn right, down a broad, sandy farm track, past Forester's Lodge—the home of the Edge's National Trust warden—and the National Trust's Countryside Office.

To the right are rolling fields and to the left mixed birch, oak, rowan and Scots pine woodland.

The Edge's trees are relatively new; until quite recently the ridge could boast panoramic views around the compass. In prehistoric times, the Edge was a stretch of wild moorland spangled with boggy pools and thick with heather, gorse and broom. But by 1640, beech trees, imported from the south, had been introduced to the estate by the landowner, Sir Thomas Stanley. The first groups of Scots pines were planted only in 1745.

Within 500 metres of the road, as the track bends left, take the waymarked path that rises diagonally into the woods.

Beyond the fence ahead is the open scar of the Engine Vein, where a line of early mining pits was excavated in around 1900. Scores of stone hammer heads, numerous flint tools, and an amazingly well-preserved oak spade—which was dated to the Bronze Age by the British Museum —have been discovered elsewhere on the Edge. Together, they point to extensive prehistoric mineral exploration.

From the Engine Vein, later galleries and levels reach out beneath the Edge; the total length of the underground workings here, from east to west is about 480 feet/146 metres, making them miniscule in comparison with West and Wood Mines. Nonetheless, the area is protected as a Site of Special Scientific Interest, or SSSI. In all, there are 22 miles/35 kilometres of tunnels, on several levels, beneath the Edge. Today the workings are blocked off for the safety of the public.

Alderley Edge Mines

'IN THE SPACE OF A FEW ACRES,' wrote an excited mineralologist, in 1811, *'are the ores of most of the metals found in England.'* That is not quite true; but copper, lead, iron, zinc, silver, arsenic, silicon, barium, vanadium and magnesium are all found, in a bewildering variety of forms. Most occur as thin films coating the pebbles and grains of the porous sandstone.

Alderley Edge was created millions of years ago, when a huge block, or *horst*, of sandstone was pushed up between two faults. Warm, saline solutions carrying dissolved metals then percolated along the faults and out into the surrounding rock. They are not igneous intrusions. Even at this moment minerals are being redeposited on the mine surfaces; it's a continuous process.

Four thousand years ago, Bronze Age miners were attracted to this then desolate ridge by the brightly coloured copper ores that stained the rocky surface. They extracted the ores from pits along the faults. It seems the Romans worked the copper ore and lead too; a hoard of Roman coins found in a shaft attached to the Engine Vein in 1995 helped archaeologists date the workings to the 1st century AD.

Significantly, there is no reference to the mines in Domesday; and it's likely that the hills were quiet until the seventeenth century. Between 1693 and 1879, seven different mining concerns tried their luck. Some, like The Copper Mining Company of Macclesfield, made their fortunes. Others were ruined. Then, in 1807, at the height of the Napoleonic War, the mines were revitalised by the discovery of cobalt— used to give the blue tint to porcelain, and rare in Britain. But it was a brief respite; the war ended, superior French cobalt ore became available again, and the mines closed. The Alderley Edge mines were re-opened briefly in 1865, and again during the First World War.

Victorian visitors were once enthralled by passages and caverns lit by guides with candles, flares and fireworks. But after a spate of fatalities, 'Blaster' Bates, the explosives expert and raconteur, finally sealed off the last entrances in 1964.

Return to the broad farm track and turn left. Two hundred metres on, at a meeting of paths, the track sweeps to the right towards Edge House Farm.

A large protruding sandstone block by the side of the track here is the Golden Stone, deliberately mentioned in the legend of the Wizard. The cleft rock has acted as a boundary marker, or merestone, *since time immemorial; and seems to have had some, now unintelligible, significance to the prehistoric miners.*

2. The path ahead leads to secluded Clockhouse Wood and Dickens Wood, but we turn left, through the gate, alongside the Edge.

This once broad track is the old Carriage Drive—constructed along the lip of the Edge by the local landowners, the Stanleys, so their guests could wonder at the view.

The tree-lined drive rises gently uphill, with tantalising glimpses of rolling Cheshire farmland visible between mature trees, before bursting into the open once more at Stormy Point.

One of the best known parts of Alderley Edge, Stormy Point rises 300-400 feet/90-120 metres above the Cheshire Plain. On a clear day the view encompasses the Derbyshire hills and parts of greater Manchester, with the folly of Lyme Cage visible in the middle distance; far below, black and white Friesian cattle look like toys spread out in the geometric fields.

Back from the edge is a narrow, slot-like excavation known as the 'Devil's Grave'. It cuts through the harder 'pebble bed' sandstone that protects the softer stone beneath. Walk down into the cleft and below an overhang is a broad, sloping cave, supported by brick pillars and blocked off by steel bars. A circular hole in the roof has been wisely covered in the past with a hefty stone block. The surrounding mineralised soil is sufficiently toxic that no plants can grow, and the area has been bare for centuries. Several small trial workings have been made to the east of the Devil's Grave.

A victim of its own popularity, Stormy Point has suffered from serious erosion for years. In an attempt to slow the Edge's decline, and encourage the regrowth of native heather, the National Trust have fenced off much of the slope, including the entrances to the Doc and Pillar Mines.

3. From the Devil's Grave, a path leads off, half right, beneath gnarled Scots pines and into the trees. Almost immediately, the path forks right, towards Saddle Bole. As it drops gently downhill, along the contours of the slope, huge and curious slabs of rock, like teeth, jut from the ground.

These are the Iron Gates—where the legend says the wizard led the farmer down a dark tunnel and into the earth.

Tall, majestic beeches stretch 80-100 feet/25-30 metres up to the light. If their green-grey trunks are like muscled sinews, then in contrast their exposed roots are like arthritic fingers, clutching at the earth. Numerous trial shafts and pits dot the crest of Glaze Hill, along the fault; and these excavations are regarded as among the oldest in the Alderley Edge area.

Two hundred metres on, at the end of Glaze Hill, is the pitted summit of Saddle Bole.

The first part of the name comes from an old saddle-road, or horse track, that climbed the hill at this point, while 'bole' was the old name for a wind-driven smelter. As early as the 1690s, and perhaps before, gorse and timber from the wooded slopes were used to fuel crude smelting hearths, which caught the prevailing westerly winds up on this once exposed and treeless hill.

Return to Stormy Point and turn right. Across the open ground, two paths curve back into the trees. Take the lower path that drops obliquely down a gentle slope, not the flatter, broader one marked for wheelchairs.

Roots and outcrops of rock jut from the surface as the path runs downhill.

A hundred metres down the slope, two paths cross. Turn right, downhill again, on a timber-edged path. The path curves around the side of a steep slope, beneath oaks, hollies and dark yews. A

Three small boys looking eastwards over the Cheshire Plain to the Pennines from Alderley Edge's Stormy Point in 1949

little farther on, water drops down a damp, mossy rock face and into a slab-sided stone trough.

Just around the corner is a second, oval trough, this time carved from one piece of sandstone; water trickles into it from a groove cut in the overhang above.

This is the Holy Well. It's an attractive spot, with the trough and cave behind sheltered beneath two vast beech trees. Behind the trough, in the rock face, is another supposed site for the Iron Gates where, in the legend, the wizard and the farmer entered the underworld. Even as little as a century ago there were people still living who swore they had seen the Iron Gates and that they were real!

Tall oaks and Scots pines as straight as ships' masts line the slopes as the path crosses a crude log bridge, bends to the right, and climbs steeply up a flight of timber-edged steps.

At the crest of the slope turn right at a T-junction, and follow the well-used path just below the lip of the Edge.

The shelved outcrops of barytes-rich sandstone 50 metres on are supposed to show the outlines of the Wizard's footprints—an example of the growth of the popular legend to embrace almost everything on the Edge.

Within 200 metres the path opens out at Castle Rock.

This was the most visited part of the Edge during Victorian and Edwardian times. Castle Rock may have also been used in the far distant past by Mesolithic hunters as a hunting trap over which they drove large game to their deaths; large numbers of the hunters' tiny flint blades, or 'microliths' have been found nearby. (Interestingly, these tiny flints were misinterpreted by the Victorians as 17th century gunflints, leading to the apparently obvious but wrong idea that this must once have been a Civil War lookout).

4. From Castle Rock continue on the path alongside the fence. A few metres on, at a junction of paths, don't turn left towards the road, but instead, go right, back towards the Edge. Drop down the slope alongside two stone posts and a short flight of steps. At the bottom turn left again, on a broad path that follows the contour of the slope.

Massive sandstone bluffs overhang the path; beneath the first are the remains of a Victorian bench, the panoramic view from which is now obscured by upstart oaks and scrub elder.

Further outcrops border the path; 100 metres on, as the path starts to dip downhill beyond a bend, is the Wizard's Well.

Shaded by beech and holly trees, the well is nothing more than a simple stone trough into which water drips from the mossy stone above. What makes it unusual is the legend carved into the stone above:

> *"Drink of this, and take thy fill,*
> *for the water falls by the Wizard's will."*

Trace the now eroded letters with your fingers.

Turn back and return to the bottom of the stone steps. Continue along the path that skirts the base of Castle Rock. The winding path follows the contour of the slope, keeping close to the sandstone bluff that forms the top of the Edge.

A square stone building stood on the Armada Beacon from 1779 until 1931

Look at the different coloured strata in the rock; and notice how the harder, overlying pebble beds have protected the softer sandstones beneath.

When the bluff ends, 250 metres later, the path climbs up the slope to the right, and rejoins the wider path along the lip of the Edge. Turn left, and continue past the steps that dip down towards the Holy Well. Soon a neatly walled off area that contains a roofed reservoir belonging to the Water Board appears on the right.

5. At the far corner of the drystone wall turn right, off the main path, up a shallow flight of crude steps. Follow the wall uphill. On the left-hand side, at the top, is a mound surmounted by a plaque. This is the Armada Beacon.

The Armada Beacon sits on the highest part of the Edge. At 650 feet/200 metres above sea level, for years the Beacon stood out above the trees on the western edge of the woods. Earlier still, when the Edge was a bare and treeless heath, the mound was visible for miles around The Beacon appears on Saxton's 1577 map of Cheshire; and we doubtless used to signal to the Helsby, Frodsham and Halton (Runcorn beacons the coming of the Spanish Armada in 1588. In 1779 a squar building was built on top of the mound to house a vast iron pot full of pitch that could be lit at a moment's warning. But according to loca legend, the already rickety building was blown down one wind December night in 1931.

More interesting still, it seems the high point was also special fo our distant ancestors; the underlying hillock is now recognised an protected as a Bronze Age burial mound. No record of any archaeologica excavation exists; perhaps the cremated ashes of some long dead chieftai lie silently in their burial urn in the dark earth beneath your feet.

From the Beacon's summit, head straight on, downhill, on well-used path. At the base of the slope, take the broader, le hand fork of the path; it's smoothly surfaced and waymarked a suitable for wheelchairs.

Go straight ahead at the crossroad of major paths. Beyon the deep sandstone cleft of the Engine Vein, the path bends t the right, then slopes downhill, back towards the Wizard of Edg restaurant, Wizard Tearooms and National Trust car park.

But before you leave, pause to consider the secret world hidde beneath your feet. Deep under the Edge, mile upon mile of ancien tunnels snake away into the darkness. Connected by a twisted logic these galleries, shafts and levels create an often deadly three dimensiona maze. Now the only ways in are those made by the Derbyshire Cavin Club. The underworld was never for the public; and so today, stee man-hole covers replace the Wizard's Iron Gates.

14. Bollington

From 'White Nancy' along Kerridge Ridge

'White Nancy', beacon site, Kerridge Stone quarries, fossils, Peaks and Plains, coal pits, and flag-stoned footpath

Start: *Kerridge near Bollington, 3 miles/5 kilometres north-east of Macclesfield. Map reference: SJ 937772.*

Distance: *3 miles/5 kilometres.*

Duration: *Allow 3 hours.*

Difficulty: *High wind-swept ridge, steep climb and descent, otherwise easy. Grassy paths along ridge, fields, bridleway. Muddy in parts but mainly dry.*

Food and Drink: *Bulls Head, Oak Lane, Kerridge. Robinsons. Terrace and beer garden. Bar snacks and evening meals. Children welcome. 01625 575522.*

Maps: *OS 1:25,000 Explorer 268 Wilmslow, Macclesfield and Congleton. OS 1:50,000 Landranger 118, Stoke-on-Trent and Macclesfield area.*

HARD STONE AND SOFT COTTON have shaped the history of Kerridge and her big sister, Bollington. Kerridge stone has been recognised since the beginning of the 16th century; while Bollington cotton rose to prominence only much later, from the late 18th century onwards.

Back in Tudor times, by the early 1500s over half of what was still called Macclesfield Forest had been enclosed: farms, sheepfolds and fields had been walled off in the valleys and on the lower slopes of the hills. *'Robert Shrigley'*, a contemporary document tells us, *'hath taken in some intakes on the King's commyn called Caroyge* [Kerridge] *... and budded a house and a chamber'*. Such colonisation of 'waste' was officially encouraged. By 1515 the Crown had leased the stone rights to Macclesfield Corporation, and stone flags from the quarries were used *'to pave all the stree* *in the Town'*. Later the haphazard pitting of the common becam dangerous. Quarrying was regulated; and in 1625 the leases wer assigned to local landowners. The pale yellow sandstone has bee prized ever since: many of Cheshire's older buildings are roofe with it—like Pott Shrigley and Siddington churches, an Prestbury's Priest's House; while the nave of Christchurcl Oxford is paved with Kerridge stone.

King cotton came later. The soft water flowing from the porou gritstones and sandstones, together with wool from the hill meant that spinning and weaving had long been importar cottage industries in the area.

But when water-driven machinery began to arrive in the 18t century, mills sprang up to replace the local craftsmen. From a essentially agricultural community of 1,200 inhabitants in 1801 Bollington had grown by 1851 to become a small industrial tow of 4,600 people. In fact, so many skilled Lancashire worker moved in that Bollington was described as, *'a Derbyshire town i Cheshire peopled by Lancashire folk'*. The town mills weathered slump when the supply of raw cotton dried up in 1861-65, durin the American Civil War. Only to suffer when large numbers c Bollington people emigrated to Canada in the 1870s, attractec by newspaper advertisements offering assisted-passages anc government land grants. Spurred on by low wages and poo prospects, the numbers leaving had grown to a flood by 1911– a movement halted only by the coming of the First World Wai Today the mills, many of which are listed buildings, are used fo other things.

The walk

The walk begins in Kerridge, just south of Bollington and 2 miles 3 kilometres north-east of Macclesfield. Park close to the Bull Head on Oak Lane, at the foot of Redway Lane.

1. Walk up the Redway to a sharp dog-leg bend at the top wher Redway Lane becomes Windmill Lane. Standing literally at th north end of Kerridge Ridge, this is known as Northend.

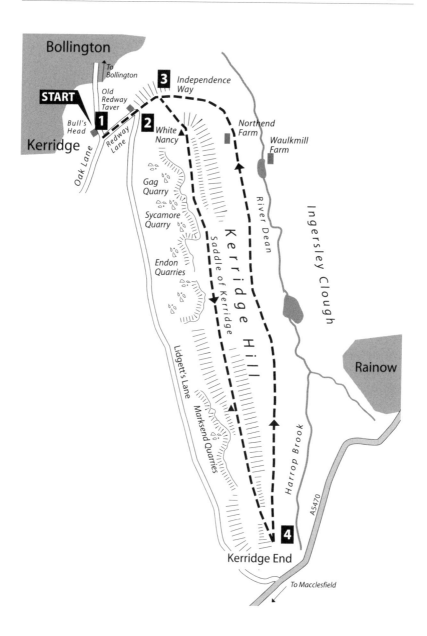

Bollington

To Bollington

START

Old Redway Taver

Bull's Head

Kerridge

Oak Lane

Redway Lane

3 Independence Way

1

2 White Nancy

Gag Quarry

Sycamore Quarry

Endon Quarries

Lidgett's Lane

Marksend Quarries

Saddle of Kerridge

K e r r i d g e   H i l l

River Dean

Northend Farm

Waulkmill Farm

I n g e r s l e y   C l o u g h

Rainow

Harrop Brook

A5470

4

Kerridge End

To Macclesfield

White Nancy

'WHITE NANCY', AS THE MONUMENT IS KNOWN, has been variously described as a sugar-loaf (sugar was once sold in large, pointed lumps), as a bishop's mitre, and as a lady in a long white cloak. It is said to stand on the site of a far older beacon. Built of whitewashed stone, it was erected by the Gaskell family of nearby Ingersley Hall early in the nineteenth century to commemorate the Battle of Waterloo.

Originally it was a kind of drystone summerhouse with a door and a circular stone table and bench inside. Bollington folklore tells how, a century or so ago, local lads rolled the circular table down the hill on its edge; on the way down it sliced through a house: in through the back wall and out through the front! Luckily, no one was killed; but it took a team of six horses to drag the tabletop back to the summit. Squire Gaskell left two shillings and sixpence per year in his will to whitewash the beacon; sadly, constant vandalism meant that the doorway was eventually walled up.

A more inventive version of how 'White Nancy' got its name appears in a Victorian guide. John Gaskell apparently had the beacon built to guide home one of his brothers who had gone abroad. It's said that when his ship docked, he could see the monument all the way from Liverpool.

White Nancy soon became a symbol for Bollington. Bonfires were lit on the hilltop near the Nancy to celebrate Queen Victoria's jubilees in 1887 and 1897; and to mark the coronations of Edward VII in 1902 and George V in 1911. A far bigger fire was caused by accident in the summer of 1911. After a long drought, the gorse was set alight one Sunday evening, and flames leapt high into the air, illuminating the ridge. The next morning revealed that little actual damage had been done; but the free spectacle was long remembered.

This 1930s' photo of White Nancy shows the folly before its door was blocked up and the monument painted white

Until recently, the pair of stone houses on the apex of the bend was the white-painted Redway Tavern. Like the Bull's Head, Redway Tavern was bought, together with a few acres of rough grazing, by local Heaver's Brewery in 1905; in those days publicans often supplemented their income with part-time farming. Both pubs, too, were popular with Kerridge quarrymen; and both were sometimes the scene of inquests into the accidental deaths of quarrymen.

The row of five cottages to the left of the old pub was known as 'Tuppence Ha'penny Row', because the rent of each at one time was a halfpenny a week.

2. To the right of the old pub on the bend, a public footpath leads uphill, beneath a tunnel of wild-cherry and sycamore trees.

Generations of quarrymen and stonemasons have worked the quarries on Kerridge Ridge. In this early photograph, much of the work is still being done by hand

A sign warns 'Private. No Through Road. Footpath Only'. Now surfaced with deeply scored concrete, the steep lane was once called Betty's Brew. At the top of the slope the lane bends to the right, crosses a cattle grid, and levels out on Independence Way.

The track is waymarked as part of the Gritstone Trail and leads on to Northend Farm.

3. But instead we climb steeply up a winding flight of cleverly 'pitched' stone steps to the right. The pitched stone path ascends steeply towards the summit. Outcrops of Kerridge Stone jut from the grassy slope, alongside some of the older quarries on the ridge. This is the steepest part of the whole walk, and is sometimes muddy.

But the sight of one of Cheshire's most curious landmarks looming over the brow of the ridge draws the climber upward.

The view from the monument is impressive too; which isn't surprising at 290 metres/920 feet above sea level. Beyond the valley-

bottom town of Bollington, with its canal, and mills and houses all built from Kerridge stone, are Nab Head and the long scar of Moorside Quarry; and to the left the wide panorama of the Cheshire Plain. It's fascinating to identify landmarks from up here with the aid of map and compass. Look for the white disc of Jodrell Bank radio telescope and the distant crag of Beeston Castle.

From White Nancy, follow the drystone wall along the ridge, and go through a metal kissing gate towards a group of windswept sycamores and beeches. Kerridge Hill is a knife-edged ridge that extends almost due north-south for about 1½ miles / 2.5 kilometres, from North End to Kerridge End in the south.

The name Kerridge first appears in records in 1467 as Caryge, *from the Old English words,* caeg *meaning stone and* hrycg *meaning ridge or back. Similarly,* cerrig *in Celtic Welsh means simply, stone. An important down-throw fault—a crack in the earth's surface—runs along the western flank of the ridge from Bollington towards the North Staffordshire coalfield. Along this fault the gritstones of the Peaks have pushed underneath the Carboniferous sandstones of Kerridge and buckled them upwards.*

Beyond the trees, go through a second metal kissing gate and on along the ridge.

Centuries of quarrying have eaten at the western edge, and the ground falls away sharply on either side. To the right is disused Gag Quarry; now invaded by sycamore saplings, the old workings are over 25 metres/80 feet deep. To the left, beech and larch trees huddle on the leeward side of the ridge.

For a while, dense brambles and gnarled hawthorns protect the path from the wind. A hundred and fifty metres or so beyond the trees, the path runs above Sycamore Quarry.

Below, the growl of huge mechanical diggers is punctuated by the high, ringing notes of hammer and chisel as skilled craftsmen split the pale sandstone; the finished roofing slabs are piled in steel boxes. Cranes angle out over the exposed rock faces. Sycamore Quarry still produces crazy paving, drystone walling, and dressing-stone for suburban gardens.

But the scene was not always so ordered. On the 14th of September 1777, the quarries were shaken by a violent earthquake centred o Macclesfield. 'Fair and fine, wind east, but very mild and hot wrote a local farmer. He continued, 'At a few minutes before eleve I was attending divine service in church when occured a mos sudden and violent trembling of the floor, which encreasin shooke the whole fabrick in a terrable manner, so that the churc was expected to fall and burie us all.' Luckily for Kerridge, it was Sunday. Had it happened on a weekday, the tremor would have kille most, if not all, of the quarrymen.

Above Sycamore Quarry, go through another kissing gate an continue along the ridge, now with the drystone wall once mor on your left. Three hundred metres on, the path breasts a sligh rise, then drops down into the Saddle of Kerridge.

To the right of this hollow in the ridge, a wire fence carrie notices that warn: *'Danger. Fenced Quarry Face. Keep Well Clear* Disused Endon Quarries, far below, are now used as a shootin range.

Continue along the ridge for 200 metres, keeping the drystor wall to your left. At a signpost for the Gritstone Trail, turn lef over a stile and through a metal gate. From here, our path split off from the Gritstone Trail. While the Trail drops away, downhi to the left, we continue upwards, to the summit of the ridge, 32 metres, or well over 1,000 feet, above sea level.

At the top of the slope, the wind combs the wiry grass, an low hawthorns crouch, black against the eastern flank of the hil Now only 3 metres/10 feet wide, the ridge narrows, carryin the path along its spine.

At the crest of the slope, go through another kissing gate an continue on along the ridge.

The views to east and west are in complete contrast. The tw landscapes—each determined by its underlying geology—are starkl different. To the left, the Peaks are a maze of drystone walls; to th right, the green Cheshire fields are framed by hedges. To the east th panorama is mainly agricultural, while industry scars the wester view. Sheep nibble the Peaks' undulating hills; while cattle browse on Cheshire's flat, flat Plains. For want of a subtler metaphor, the landscapes are as alike as chalk and cheese.

Some 250 metres on is a white-painted OS triangulation point —a concrete base from which to take the bearings used in map making. It also marks the highest point on the ridge. Far to the south, the view embraces the outlines of the Wrekin and Wenlock Edge, away in Shropshire. Hanging in the air like fragments of torn black cloth, crows tumble over the edge.

Beyond the 'trig' point, go through another metal kissing gate. Suddenly, the ridge falls away and the view opens out. The path drops away along the slope of the ridge. Grass-softened pits of older stone workings dot the pasture.

To the right is Marksend Quarry. Below, large-wheeled diggers and yellow Hy-Macs with jack-hammers on the end of their hydraulic arms move about among the cutting sheds. The stone is pale and very hard; yet it splits easily along the bedding planes, and so has long been popular as a roofing material. Interestingly, Carboniferous fossils are sometimes found in the rock: shells, and sea-bed worm tracks and ripple marks. Look closely at the drystone wall beside the path: beneath the lichen the stone is pale yellow, and the bedding planes are well defined.

At the bottom of the grassy slope, the path kinks to the right, and drops between yellow-flowered, coconut-scented gorse bushes into a shallow, long disused quarry.

Notice how close to the surface the rock is, and how the nutrient-poor soil is as shallow as a tarpaulin draped across the ridge. The huge blocks of stone on the quarry floor also show clearly the strata of the bedding planes.

Leave the old quarry through a gap in the drystone wall and narrow gate. Beyond, a broad incline descends the hill, falling gently across the contours of the slope.

Banked up by retaining drystone walls, it once carried the quarried stone away, downhill, probably in trucks mounted on a narrow-gauge railway.

4. At the bottom of the slope—yet still a hundred feet or so above the valley floor—the track levels out beneath a row of tall ash and sycamores. But we double back here to the left, at an acu angle, along a bridleway that skirts the base of Kerridge Hi From here, the route turns north, tracing the contour of the slop

Beyond the fence to the right, cattle pastures fall away to Harr Brook, a tributary stream of the River Dean.

Soon the path goes through a metal gate, and runs betwee gorse and hawthorn. Cut into the slope, the track is old and we defined.

Where the path divides, continue on the broader, upp bridleway.

The path runs on above mixed deciduous woodland.

Until the 1990s, this was the site of the derelict Cow Lane Mi with its distinctive tall square chimney. Originally a silk mill, an then a bleach works, the ruins of the water-powered mill were hidd. among trees beside the River Dean. The village of Rainow, whose nan in Anglo-Saxon meant 'Raven Hill', once had 24 mills; all have no been demolished.

Through another horse-sized wooden gate beside a ladd stile, the path runs on across the field, dropping fractionally dow the contours of the slope.

At the bottom of the field, go through another broad, old gate between stone gateposts. For a while, our route rejoins th Gritstone Trail as it drops down from the ridge.

Beyond another field gate, the path rises slightly above plantation of mature mixed conifers sheltering Kerridgesic House.

Above the path, high on Kerridge Hill's eastern slopes, coal w. once dug from opencast drift mines and stone-lined shafts. It w. dangerous and gruelling work, despite the use of donkeys to winch th coal to the surface. Packhorses with panniers carried the coal away fuel the first steam-powered mills. Traces of fossil fish have been foun in the old workings.

Past the plantation a small gate leads out onto open sheep

Several footpaths around Kerridge Hill are paved with flagstones. It's a fine unique local feature

slopes. Now gradually being overgrown with grass, sections of the path across the field are still paved with Kerridge slabs—a uniquely local feature and a reminder of the days when everyone walked to work.

Beneath a band of mature deciduous woodland, the path goes through a narrow gateway between two stone uprights. From here it heads out across the fields, where mushrooms grow, keeping 50 metres or so above the woodland edge along Ingersley Clough. Don't take the lower path that slants downhill and into the trees. Soon, tall ashes from an old hedgerow line the route; and the instantly recognisable shape of White Nancy tops the ridge up to the left ahead.

At the far side of the field, go over a stile and then immediately right and left, past a securely fenced enclosure protecting ornamental ducks and chickens, to skirt below North End Farm.

Before the First World War the eleven-strong Barlow family worked the farm; then seven sons and a daughter emigrated to Canada. Two of the boys were killed in the war. One son and a daughter returned to Bollington; but the others stayed in Canada where they prospered.

Beyond the farm, go through a gate and on uphill to the left along Independence Way. The farm drive continues around the end of the ridge, with White Nancy high on the hillside above. Stretched out below is the mill town of Bollington. Go over two cattle grids 250 metres apart, and then curve downhill to the left on Betty's Brew, and so back to the Redway and the Bulls Head on Oak Lane.

It's a curious corner of Cheshire, more Peaks than Plains. Yet for generations of Kerridge people, their lives shaped by the harsh demands of cotton and stone, it has been home. Perhaps even for those who emigrated and never returned.

Further Reading

	The View from the Hill: Burwardsley—The History of a Cheshire Village, Burwardsley Millennium Book, 1992
Bullock, JD	*Pre-Conquest Cheshire 383-1066*, Chester, 1972.
Coward, TA	*Cheshire*, Cambridge, 1910.
Coward, TA	*Cheshire Traditions and History*, Methuen, 1932
Crossley, Fred H	*Cheshire*, London, 1949.
Crump, WB	*Saltways from the Cheshire Wiches*, TLCAS, Vol LIV, 1939.
Dawson, Greg	*Wyrale: Wirral Topics,* Dawson Publishing (Irby), 1996.
Dodgson, J McN.	*The Place Names of Cheshire*, Vols I-IV, Cambridge, 1970.
Driver, JL	*Cheshire in the Later Middle Ages*, Chester, 1971
Dutton, RJ	*Hidden Highways of Cheshire*, published by Gordon Emery, Chester, 1999.
Harris, BE (Ed.)	*The Victoria County History of Cheshire*, Vol II, Oxford, 1979.
Hughes, Herbert	*Cheshire and its Welsh Border*, London, 1966.
Husain, BMC	*Cheshire under the Norman Earls*, Chester, 1973
	Kelly's Directory of Cheshire, Annually.
Latham, Frank	*Tiverton*, Family History Society of Cheshire
Ormerod, G	*The History of the County Palatine and City of Chester*, Three Vols., 2nd Edition, ed. by T Helsby, 1882.
Richards, Raymond	*Old Cheshire Churches*, London, 1947.
Stephens, WB (Ed.)	*History of Congleton*, Manchester, 1970.
Sylvester, D and Nutty, G	*The Historical Atlas of Cheshire*, Cheshire Community Council, 1958.

Thompson, FH	*Roman Cheshire*, Chester, 1964.
Varley, WJ	*Cheshire Before the Romans*, Chester, 1964.
Varley, WJ	*Recent Investigations into the Origins of Cheshire Hillforts*, TLCAS. Vol. LI, 1936.
Watkins, WT	*Roman Cheshire*, Liverpool, 1886.

About the Author

Tony Bowerman is a heritage and countryside interpretation consultant whose clients include The National Trust, English Heritage, Cadw and the RSPB; for details see: www.heritageinterpretation.co.uk.

He also publishes tourist guides under the Wordplay imprint—www.wordplaypublishing.co.uk—and is a director of Northern Eye Books Limited. He lives with his wife and three children in Tattenhall, Cheshire.